Bennett Books
Spiritual Classics Editions

BENNETT BOOKS *Spiritual Classics Editions* are reprints of works that support spiritual development. For those who sincerely seek the "real world of human existence," they will be of lasting value. In the fullest sense, they are "Work" books—giving practical guidance for deepening our understanding of the human condition, for continuing along our paths of transformation, and for acquiring in ourselves an enduring relationship to the spiritual world.

Each *Spiritual Classics Edition* features Smyth-sewn binding and acid-free paper.

D1602464

G.I. Gurdjieff, circa 1924

Is There "Life" on Earth?

An Introduction to Gurdjieff

○

IS THERE "LIFE" ON EARTH? is a series of four lectures, first delivered by J.G. Bennett at Denison House, London, on October 3, 10, 17 and 24, 1949, under the name "Gurdjieff—The Making of a New World."

Lecture 2 (Chapter 2), "Gurdjieff—The Man and his Work," was rewritten by Bennett in 1973 to include an account taken from a biographical note prepared by some of Gurdjieff's older pupils at the request of his American publishers.

The lectures have been otherwise revised only so that the tenses accurately reflect Gurdjieff's death, which occurred on October 29, 1949, a few days after the presentation of the final lecture.

Is There "Life" on Earth?

An Introduction to Gurdjieff

J.G. Bennett

BENNETT BOOKS

Santa Fe, New Mexico

First published in 1973 by Stonehill Publishing Company

BENNETT BOOKS
P.O. Box 1553
Santa Fe, New Mexico 87504

Printed in the United States of America
95 94 93 92 91 90 89   5 4 3 2 1
First Bennett Books Edition 1989

Cover photo: photographer unknown. G.I. Gurdjieff, circa 1924.
Cover design: **AM Services,** Santa Fe, New Mexico.

Frontispiece photo: courtesy of Peter Swales.

Library of Congress Cataloguing-in-Publication Data

Bennett, John G. (John Godolphin), 1897-1974.
[Introduction to Gurdjieff]
Is there "life" on earth? : an introduction to Gurdjieff /
J.G. Bennett. — 1st Bennett Books ed.
p.   cm. — (A Bennett Books spiritual classic)
Reprint. Originally published: An introduction to Gurdjieff.
New York : Stonehill Pub. Co., 1973
Slightly rev. lectures originally delivered at Denison House, London,
October 1949, under title: Gurdjieff, the man and his work.
ISBN 0-9621901-1-X (pbk. : alk. paper) : $9.50
1. Gurdjieff, Georges Ivanovitch, 1872-1949.   I. Title.   II. Series.
B4249.G84B4665   1989
197—dc20
[B]   89-38486
CIP

Contents

REFLECTIONS OF THE REAL WORLD

BENNETT BOOKS dedicates this publication to all those who have a genuine concern for the fate of our planet Earth and who are thereby moved to seek *real* and lasting solutions to the problems arising from the deteriorating conditions of life hereon.

Bennett Books publishes material that reflects the work of those who, from their deep concern for the fate of humanity, have penetrated the "real world" of human existence.

—The Publisher

"WE ARE NOW in a period of transition to a New Epoch; and new illusions are arising to replace the old ones."

Fallen Leaves

A collection of J.G. Bennett's writings, lectures and letters.

Foreword

THE THEME OF THESE LECTURES, given 40 years ago, is as important now as it was then: that the world is in a period of great change, which is reaching a critical stage, and mankind must learn how to cooperate with the processes of change or risk "bringing the temple down around his ears." As J.G. Bennett makes very clear in this book, the value of Gurdjieff's message is that it not only offers an explanation of the whole cosmic drama and the part humanity has to play in it, but it tells us *how* we can play that part and acquire something valuable for ourselves.

This "how" is especially significant. Even people with a short-term view of human affairs and with no interest in what can be broadly described as "spiritual matters" can see that beneath the temporary and beguiling easing of human problems in some parts of the world, the underlying situation is highly unstable and increasingly hazardous. What is rarely seen, however, is the real reason for this state of affairs and what can be done about it. Gurdjieff's teaching is, above all, practical—it is here to be used.

Those who have read Bennett's later writings, or who have studied with him at the school he set up in 1971 at Sherborne in England, will recognize this theme of a world in transition and the part we must play in seeing it through. In his Introduction to the first publication of these lectures, written on Gurdjieff's birthday 23 years after they were first given, Bennett reiterates that theme, stressing the unique and vital contribution of Gurdjieff's ideas—he no doubt would have done the same for this new edition.

Today, as we enter the closing decade of the 20th century, the state of affairs of life on earth makes it even more timely to examine Gurdjieff's message. Bennett, at the end of his second lecture, presents it simply and to the point: "Only by the unremitting struggle of the individual for his self-perfecting can a force be created that will change the world."

1

This idea of changing the world was expressed in the overall title Bennett gave these lectures when he originally presented them in 1949: *Gurdjieff—The Making of a New World*. His choice of word reveals the immense significance he placed on Gurdjieff's message: that it was a key to the creation of a "new epoch" that would replace the "old world," which was then, as it is now, visibly dying. Bennett envisaged this change taking tens, perhaps hundreds, of years, but stressed that we had to prepare for it now.

When these lectures were published in book form in 1973, he had already used the original title for a major new book* on Gurdjieff's life and work, so he renamed this volume *Is There "Life" on Earth?* Why "Life" in quotation marks, the reader may ask? Because Bennett wanted to emphasize the idea that consciousness in man is *not* assured, and that as we presently exist, we are not living in the way that is required of us.

These talks were designed as an introduction to Gurdjieff, to whet the appetite. In this they succeed; they convey much of the essence of his message in a concise form, and their tone demonstrates the degree of confidence that Bennett placed in Gurdjieff at that time.

J.G. Bennett first met Gurdjieff in Turkey in 1920, a meeting that had a revolutionary effect on the course of his life. These lectures, given in London in October 1949 after an extraordinary summer of very intense personal work with Gurdjieff, marked the start of another transformation in Bennett's life. Only five days after the last of these lectures was delivered, on October 29, Gurdjieff died. Of that event, Bennett wrote in his autobiography:** "I had lost my best friend and teacher, and I had lost him just when I most needed his help in order to make the next step." As with all of Gurdjieff's pupils, Bennett was now obliged to struggle on without a teacher. But Gurdjieff had shown him enough to make that struggle unusually fruitful; and he had left behind a great legacy for all who wished to work for their own self-perfecting.

In October 1949 arrangements had effectively been completed to publish the first series of Gurdjieff's own writings, *An Objectively Impartial Criticism of the Life of Man,* or *Beelzebub's Tales to His Grandson.* Gurdjieff so constructed his books, and in particular *Beelzebub,* that they could themselves act as a teacher for those who are prepared

---

* *Gurdjieff: Making a New World.* New York: Harper & Row Publishers, Inc., 1974.
** *Witness, The Autobiography of John G. Bennett.* Charles Town, West Virginia: Claymont Communications, 1983.

to work seriously at understanding them and wish to distill and act upon the practical information they contain. Bennett devotes the whole of the fourth lecture in this book to Gurdjieff's writings. At his International Academy for Continuous Education in Sherborne, England—a "fourth way school" based on Gurdjieff's teaching—he gave special attention to *Beelzebub's Tales to His Grandson,* personally reading it aloud each evening to his students.

At the same time, Bennett emphasized the importance of making the ideas one's own—of working with them. In the preface to *Gurdjieff: Making a New World,* published the same year these lectures first appeared in print, he writes:

> "I always have regarded Gurdjieff as my teacher, and a few days before he died, I promised that I would devote myself to making his ideas understood and accepted as far as was in my power. I felt that, in order to do that, I had to work with it and make something of it for myself."

During his efforts to "make something of it for himself," Bennett wrote a large number of books and gave numerous lectures, touching many lives. Many of his books are unfortunately now out of print. These lectures, re-printed here for the first time since 1973, are well worth studying, even if you are already familiar with the ideas they contain. If, however, they are new to you and you find, as Bennett hopes in his own introduction, that they encourage you to come closer to Gurdjieff's work, then reading *Beelzebub* itself is an indispensable part of that study.

It is important to remember, however, that Gurdjieff taught practical methods that go beyond his writings. These can effectively be undertaken only in groups—of which there are now a reasonable number—where there has been a genuine transmission of his work. Gurdjieff's writings are full of references to groups formed to work together on some or other aspect of the "unremitting struggle for self-perfecting." Something that is impossible for an individual to achieve on his own may be possible in a group. If you are about to make this transition, I hope this book will be a point of departure.

—George Bennett
Cave Junction, Oregon
July 1989

"TWO THINGS have no limit:
the stupidity of man and the
mercy of God."
—G.I. Gurdjieff

Introduction

FOR AT LEAST TEN THOUSAND YEARS, from the end of the Ice Age, the people of Central Asia were the active core of the human race. When India and the Far East, all of Europe and all of Africa except Abyssinia and what is now the Sahara Desert were still in the hunting and fruit-gathering cultures of the Stone Age, the Aryan, Turanian and Semitic people of Central Asia had highly developed societies and possessed knowledge of man, his nature and his true destiny that has never been surpassed. The region was protected by mountains on all sides, to which about 7,000 years ago the deserts of Gob, Kizil and Kara Kum added further impediments to travel. The land was fertile and the climate envigorating, and wave after wave of conquest and civilization have come from it through the millennia. Only a handful of travellers like Marco Polo, Ibn Battuta and Ch'ang Ch'un dared the perils of travelling through the mountains and brought back accounts of the high civilizations they found, but even they did not penetrate to the sanctuaries where the ancient wisdom was preserved. These were hidden in the great limestone caves of the Syr Darya and the Pianje rivers, in the remote valleys of the Pamirs and the Hindu Kush, and in the oases of the Gobi and Takla Makam deserts. It was not until the 18th century that the Russians began to penetrate from the West and systematically destroy the old cultures.

Towards the end of the 19th century, Helena Petrovna Blavatsky, co-founder of the Theosophical Society, claimed to have penetrated beyond Tibet and reached the sanctuaries of the "Masters of Wisdom." Her books *The Secret Doctrine* and *Isis Unveiled** showed familiarity with the Tantric Buddhism of Tibet, but not of the far more remarkable teachings preserved in Central Asia. Nevertheless, her books and her personality aroused a deep and lasting interest in the belief that there are "Masters" who influence the destiny of mankind from "Shambala," the supposed center of the earth's spiritual activity. Many travellers have tried unsuccessfully to trace the sources she claimed to have discovered, but little that was convincing came out until Gurdjieff appeared on the European scene soon after World War I. When one his pupils, P. D. Ouspensky, began to lecture in London and Gurdjieff soon after set up his Institute [for the Harmonious Development of Man] in Paris, it was quickly recognized by students of esoteric and spiritual teachings that something new and astonishing had reached us from the East.

I was one of the few who had known Gurdjieff before he came to Europe, for I first met him in Constantinople in 1920. I was already deeply interested in Central Asia and had met many Sarts, Uzbegs and Turkmens on their way through Constantinople, among whom were Sufi sheikhs who were not ordinary men. Gurdjieff was in a class by himself. All of us who met him then soon realized that he must have penetrated more deeply than any previous travellers of the 19th and 20th centuries into the secrets of the Masters of Wisdom. Since then more than 50 years have passed, and more and more people are realizing that he had a message of real value to the modern world.

Gurdjieff was born on December 28, 1877**. By the time he was 11, he had shown unusual psychic gifts and had already decided to devote his life to finding an answer to the question "What is the sense and purpose of life on the earth and in particular of human life?" His early searches took him to Crete and the Holy Land, to Egypt, Abyssinia and Mesopotamia, to Kurdistan and Northwest Persia. From 1898 onwards he concentrated his

---

* Wheaton, IL: Theosophical Publishing House, 1980 and 1971 respectively.
** [The exact date of Gurdjieff's birth is disputed. In practice, his followers celebrate it on January 13th. Bennett and his students also celebrated it on this day.]

search in Turkestan and the regions north of Tibet as far as China and Tibet itself.

In the course of his travels, he found traces of traditions thousands of years old and was able to enter and live in communities that were custodians of the traditions. He told us that he had met men over 200 years old and in full possession of their faculties. He witnessed temple dances and rituals through which the ancient wisdom had been preserved. After many years of search, he arrived unexpectedly at one of the sanctuaries of the Sarman Brotherhood that was founded in Babylon at the time of Sargon the Great—that is, 4500 years ago—and was initiated into their secrets. During his time in Abyssinia and Egypt, he had been able to decipher secrets of the Egyptian mysteries from the time before the Sphinx was buried in sand. In short, he was privileged to receive help and instruction from masters of wisdom of whose very existence very few people are aware.

By the year 1909 his period of search was coming to an end, and he set himself to find means of putting all he had learned and discovered for himself into a form that would make it accessible to ordinary people under the changed conditions of the modern world. In 1911 Gurdjieff set up his own center in Tashkent, the ancient Yesi. It is a remarkable tribute to the standing he had already acquired that he was accepted as a new spiritual teacher in a place within reach of the great Syrdaryan caves and valleys that for thousands of years had been the home of the Masters of Wisdom. He remained in Tashkent for two years, during which time he convinced himself that his "system" would help people of many different types and races.

He then decided to move to the West and chose Moscow, where he already had connections. He himself declared that this decision was taken in agreement with the masters of a certain brotherhood, who undertook to train helpers selected by him for the projected dissemination of his ideas. In Russia he was received in the highest circles, even being presented to Tzar Nicholas, of whom he always spoke in affectionate and admiring terms.

His plans were delayed by the First World War and completely upset by the Russian Revolution. He went to the Caucasus and made a fresh start in Tiflis. He finally decided to abandon Asia and went to Constantinople in 1920, where I met him for the first time. He went on to Europe and founded his Institute for the Harmonious Development of Man at the Château du Prieuré south of Paris. I spent some time at the Institute in 1923 and had personal experience of his amazing psychic powers as well as of his profound knowledge of the laws of the universe and the nature of man.

He went to the U.S.A. in January 1924, when his lectures and demonstrations of temple dances and "sacred gymnastics" attracted much attention in the press and brought him both pupils and money. There was, however, little grasp of what it all signified. This was as much due to his strange behavior as to the novelty and difficulty of his ideas.

He had spoken to me in 1923 of his great plan to found branches of his Institute as well as small centers for study in all the chief countries of the West. I think he would have pursued this plan but for a nearly fatal automobile accident on July 6, 1924, soon after his return from America.

He then set himself to express his ideas and convey his methods through books. The next 10 years, from 1925 to 1935, were largely spent in writing.

Meanwhile, I had accepted him as my teacher, and this relationship remained unchanged to the end of his life. I saw a great deal of him in 1948 and 1949, both in Paris and in New York. The lectures that form the present book were delivered only a week or two before his death in 1949. I last saw him on Sunday, October 23, and spoke to him about the last lecture of the series that I was due to give the next day. He said that he counted upon the publication of his writings to spread his ideas far more widely than hitherto. He had given me copies of all the manuscripts. It was obvious to me that he had prolonged his life at the cost of great suffering in order to make sure that his books would not only be published but made freely and widely available. Having failed in his great plan for establishing a worldwide organization based on the principles of the "fourth way," Gurdjieff counted upon his writings to do the work for him after his death. The First Series, under the title *All and Everything*,* was published a few months later. The Second Series, *Meetings With Remarkable Men*,** came out in 1957. The Third Series is now being prepared for publication.***

The passage I am going to quote comes in the introduction to Book I of the Third Series, *Life is real only then, when "I am,"* and shows Gurdjieff's intentions in writing it. He writes:

> Soon after I had chosen for myself this kind of activity as the most corresponding to my unexpectedly arisen physical state, that is to say, the profession of a writer, and when, parallel to the improving of my physical state, I clearly understood that, due to certain written explanations, namely my personal ones, there will arise for the majority of contemporary people, as well as for the future generation, a great benefit; this series of books was also predetermined by me to acquit myself consciously with Great Nature for my arising and existence, chiefly for an existence not merely as an "ordinary-life," automatically fulfilling something necessary for general realizations of Great Nature, but as a determinate, conscious existence, impartially valuing itself and, besides, gifted with the capacity for an all-round perfecting, independent unity....
>
> For the readers of this series of my exposings, no matter to which degree of consciousness they should rank themselves, in my opinion it would not be superfluous to know among other things, from which of my conceptions and instinctive suppositions derived the sentence used by me above "to-acquit-myself-with-Great-Nature."
>
> This sentence which almost involuntarily burst forth

---

* [*All and Everything: An Objectively Impartial Criticism of the Life of Man, or Beelzebub's Tales to His Grandson*. New York: Harcourt, Brace & Company, Inc., 1950; E. P. Dutton & Co., Inc., 1964.]

** New York: E. P. Dutton & Co., Inc., 1963.

*** [The long-awaited Third Series was finally published nearly fifty years after it was written:*Life is real only then, when "I am,"* New York: E.P. Dutton & Co., Inc., 1981.]

from me, arose and taking a shape derived from the totality of my instinctive and conscious convictions, that by
this act, that is to say, by exposing this third and last series of my writings, that I rely and hope to fulfill: firstly,
the chiefest, in my opinion, duty of a man who has
reached responsible age and that consists in preparing in-
fallibly for posterity, according to one's individuality, certain profitable instructions; secondly, to justify worthily—
this latter quite subjectively—the sense of all my past intentional labours and conscious renunciations of all kinds
of benefits, crystallised generally in the life of contemporary people, which have always been very easily obtaina-
ble for me; and finally, thirdly, in the moment of my last
breathing, to experience with no possible mental, sensitive or instinctive doubt the impulse, sacred for a man,
that was called by the ancient Esseis* "the-impartial-self-
satisfaction."**

This was written in Paris in 1933, when Gurdjieff's hopes of re-
establishing his Institute were crumbling. When I was giving the
lectures in London, I did not know what Gurdjieff intended to do
with this unfinished work. Forty years later this "edifyingly-
instinctive" series of writings is to become available to all seekers.

The four lectures that at the time I called "Gurdjieff—The Making of a New World" cannot be published under that title because
it has already been registered for another book. The lectures
themselves are fundamentally unchanged. I was naturally very
tempted to rewrite them in the light of the extensive researches I
have made into Gurdjieff's early life and the sources of his teaching, which resulting work will shortly be published,*** and also
with hindsight of what has happened in the years since he died. I

* The manuscript reads "Esseis." This may be an error for either Essenes or
Essevis, a Sufi community that has existed in Central Asia for 900 years.
[Author's note.]
** [The passage Bennett quotes here is from his own personal copy of the then
(1973) unpublished manuscript.]
*** [*Gurdjieff: Making A New World.* Harper & Row, 1974.]

resisted this temptation, because they express what many of us were feeling at the time. We could not imagine that Gurdjieff was so soon to leave us. He was planning to revive his Institute at a château near Paris and intended to go to America to raise the money required. He was already selecting people to live there. He was so adept at hiding his real feelings that I cannot tell if he knew that death was imminent or if he thought he could once again call upon his extraordinary powers to prolong his life. It may be that the decision was not taken until a week before the end.

Gurdjieff's message is clear. The human predicament cannot be resolved by exhortation or organization. It is no use telling us what to do if we cannot do it. It is equally useless to set up organizations whose members do not even know what has to be done. The way out is through the transformation of individuals, who in their turn can guide and help mankind through the perils ahead. If we wish to take our part in this work, we must be prepared to not only make sacrifices but to make intelligent sacrifices. It is not enough to be willing—we must also learn *"how to be."* We must set ourselves to understand the "sense and purpose of our existence" and then devote ourselves to its realization. For both stages, we need to know *how*. My hope in publishing these four lectures is that they may encourage those who have come in contact with Gurdjieff at second or third hand to come closer to his work. It is now 52 years since I first met him, and I am more than ever convinced that he has a message of hope for this distressed world.

—J.G. Bennett
Sherborne House
Sherborne, Gloucestershire, England
January 13, 1973

TAKE THE UNDERSTANDING of the East
and the knowledge of the West—
and then seek.

—An aphorism inscribed in a special script above the walls
of the Study House at Gurdjieff's Institute for the
Harmonious Development of Man, Château du Prieuré,
near Fontainebleau, France.

Chapter 1

The Needs
of a
New Epoch

TO ENABLE ME TO COME QUICKLY TO GRIPS with the task I have set myself in these four lectures, I propose to take for granted that we are passing through a period of transition in human history when in some sense an old world is dying and when, therefore, in some sense a new world must be born. You may conceive of this transition as a relatively commonplace change from one set of social and material conditions of life to another. I shall ask you to let me assume that an event far more extraordinary is taking place—nothing less than the end of an epoch that has lasted for several thousand years and the heralding of a new epoch in which human existence will be quite different from anything mankind can remember.

It is in this extreme sense that I originally chose as the title of this series of lectures "The Making of a New World." I linked this with the name of "Gurdjieff," and my aim is to show you why I am convinced that it is in his teaching that the seeds of a new world are to be found.

First, we must agree as to the material of which such seeds are made. Here again, I shall spare you a long discussion and say, without attempting to prove it, that it is in the inner world of man, that is, by ideas, and not in his outer world, that is, by organization, that the life of man is changed. Obviously, not every idea has power to change our lives. It is said that what a man thinks, that he becomes. Like so many pithy sayings, this contains much that is true but also much risk of misunderstanding.

13

In one sense, it is only too painfully true. If I allow myself weak, idle thoughts, I shall become a weak, idle man. If I allow myself thoughts that are egoistic, jealous and self-centered, I shall become an egoistic, jealous, self-centered man. Every meanness, every self-indulgence and every violent impulse that take root in my inner world will sooner or later find expression in my outer manifestations. Unfortunately, the converse is not true. I do not find that if I think noble thoughts or entertain fine projects in my mind they have a corresponding effect on my behavior. I may decide to do admirable things and yet find that, however much I may think about them, they do not get done.

We must therefore distinguish between the thoughts that act upon us while we remain passive and the thoughts that become effective only insofar as we ourselves give them force. We are enslaved by the thoughts that correspond to our weaknesses. If we allow ourselves to live in daydreams, we inevitably become idlers and dreamers. But if we want to achieve, it is not sufficient to think. We have also to put force into our thoughts. This is true not only for each of us as individuals, but also in the larger affairs of the world. We see the operation of both kinds of thoughts. Suspicious, grasping, fearful thoughts—these engender fear, suspicion and grasping behavior in groups of people and in the nations of the world. We also see very good intentions expressed and thought about very earnestly, but no corresponding results in the life of communities or the policies of nations.

If, then, it is not sufficient to have "good" ideas in order to achieve "good" results, how can ideas be the seeds of a new and better world? If we can find the answer to this question, we shall have learned one of the most important secrets of human destiny. History teaches us that the world is not changed by ethical precepts, however convincing to the mind. Nor in the long run does the arousing of moral emotions, however powerful in their immediate effect, give a permanent new direction to the course of human life.

I shall take one of the most fundamental of the ideas that have in various ways influenced the life of man. This is the idea of

choice: that man is a being who is not, or at least need not be, a
mere automaton, but a being who can contribute in some way
to the determination of his own destiny. This is a very big idea,
and if it is valid, it represents the most important distinguishing
mark of a *man* as compared with a thing, or even an animal, in
whom such a power does not reside. To have the power of
choice is to be responsible, not only for ourselves but also for
the effect of our actions upon other people.

As an abstract idea, the responsibility of man is usually taken
for granted, and most people would hold without question that
it is applicable to them. Combining this with what I said about
the noble thoughts that do not issue in noble actions, you will
understand that the abstract idea that we are beings endowed
with the power of choice is not sufficient to produce a change in
our lives. If we can choose to do what is right and wise, it is
very strange that we do it so seldom. A sincere reflection on human behaviour is enough to convince us that the power of
choice plays much less part in the life of man than we think. It is
very important that we should recognize and face this fact and
try to understand its causes. They lie in the absence of force and
urgency in our attitude towards choice.

If we look at the form in which the conception of choice has
been put before mankind in the great religions of the world, we
can see that it is always associated with some further idea that
brings with it a sense of urgency. We find in Deuteronomy, "I
have set before you life and death, blessing and cursing: choose,
therefore, life that thou and thy seed may live." Here, the idea of
choice is associated with that of life and death for ourselves and
our children.

You will see at once how great is the difference between as-
serting that man is free, and therefore responsible for his actions, and setting before him the choice between life and death.
In the passage I have just quoted, choice refers to this visible life
only and to the future of mankind. In the teaching of Gotama
Buddha the idea of causality occupies a central place, and man
is represented as the slave of cause and effect, unless by his
own choice he seeks and wins his own liberation. To be the

slave of causality is to be condemned to unending suffering. He who sees this and chooses to be free can win a state of bliss that is beyond description. In the Christian Gospels, choice is expressed in a still stronger form as that between the gaining or losing of eternal life.

I have cited these few examples to show how the idea of choice is reinforced in the great religious teachings. It is because of this added power that they have been able to change the course of history.

We can see from the history of the past 200 years what happens when the idea of choice is shorn of any compelling motive. As the idea that man *must* choose degenerates into the belief that he *can* choose, and choose moreover as and when he himself wishes, it passes from a positive to a negative thought in the sense of the distinction that I made at the beginning of this lecture. If I think of my freedom as the right to satisfy my egoistic impulse and not as responsibility towards Higher Power, the whole significance of my life changes. When this degeneration is almost universal, as it has become in our time, nothing remains to prevent mankind from drifting passively towards self-destruction.

If now we look more carefully at the idea of the power of choice, we can see it can be given two entirely different meanings. In one sense, it can mean ability to choose between alternative possibilities, both on the same level—for example, selecting which make I shall choose for my new car. In the other sense, it means choosing between two different levels—for example, to choose between shirking or carrying out a difficult decision.

It is one of Gurdjieff's great contributions to the clarification of human destiny that he makes us see the distinction between real choice and illusory choice. It is an illusion to think that I can choose which make of car I shall buy, for this is determined by causes that already exist, but there is a real choice between doing and failing to do something that goes against some strong impulses of my own nature, for the doing of it implies some degree of liberation from causality.

The distinction between real and illusory choice lies deep at the root of all the great religious teachings, but it has never been made sufficiently clear. What is, however, clear and explicit in all the great religions, is their teaching that man is confronted with the choice between life and death. There are two paths before him, one the easy path that goes by itself, each step determined automatically by what has gone before. The other path is difficult and can be taken only by paying the price of effort and sacrifice. It is the distinction between the wide gate and broad way that leads to destruction and the straight gate and narrow way that leads to life.

Now, because our nature is such that a great part of each one of us is inclined to easy things, we tend to soften the sharpness of the choice. So it comes about that, in the course of time, every great teaching is watered down and weakened until it has no longer the power to make men act. When Gotama Buddha preached his doctrine of Dukkha, that is, suffering and the way to the cessation of all suffering, the idea had power and turned men's minds away from the easy doctrine of vicarious liberation through the ritual sacrifices of the Brahmins. A new force entered the world, not simply from the idea of liberation but because this idea was given force by the example of the Buddha himself and the conviction that he was able to establish in men's minds that liberation was possible and that the price, however great, was worth paying. As generation succeeded generation, Gotama became a legend. The conviction, engendered by his own demonstration, that his way could be followed lost its force in the picture of a superhuman being to whom such an achievement would be effortless, and so his life was robbed of its force as an example to ordinary men. The same has happened each time the conception of salvation, so fundamental for human destiny, has been given a new form.

Let me try to show you how an idea can have power, because if we can be clear about that, we can understand something of the conditions under which something new and effective can enter the life of man. Let me take the idea of death. I do so because it occupies a central place in Gurdjieff's teaching, and he has himself made use of it to demonstrate the very point I wish to make. The idea of death is a very big idea and one from which there is no escape. We are all of us mortal, and we all know that we must die. The idea of our mortality might therefore be expected in some way to affect our lives, but we know from our own experience and from all we see around us that, on the whole, the idea of death plays little part except on the rare occasions when we are brought close to it.

But what happens when we are brought close to it? Let us try to make a picture for ourselves. Supposing that someone very close to me, without whom I cannot imagine myself living, is not very well with a recurring fever. I decide to consult the doctor. He takes it rather seriously and advises me to go to a specialist. She goes to a specialist, as advised by the doctor, and he examines her and asks to see me and begins asking me various questions that I know are irrelevant, and, little by little, something begins to grip my heart, and I know what he is going to tell me. He tells me that she has an inoperable cancer and has twelve months to live but at the same time, that he can do something for her that can relieve her present suffering, put off the time when she will be disabled, and that she will for a number of months be able to live a normal existence. It is very important, therefore, if she is to have the utmost advantage of this respite, that she should not know about her disease, so he advises me that I should not let her know. I see in a flash the kind of future that lies before me. I must face what is going on, but at the same time I must hide it, and also I have to think that for this limited time I can no longer allow myself selfish actions and careless words that I allowed myself in the past. The memory that her death is inevitable reminds me constantly. In this way, the idea of death becomes powerful and affects my actions and enables me to do things that I could not have done before, restrain myself in things I could not have restrained myself in before.

But supposing I change the picture again a little. Supposing instead of some other person, it was I myself that was involved, and I was told, or accidentally found out or insisted on being told, that I was the one who was to die. Then a different process would have taken place. Everyone who has been in contact with many people who were dying or inevitably had to die within a certain period knows this, that although the fear of death may be present or accepted in some way outwardly, very nearly always there is an inward rejection of the idea of death, an inward feeling that somehow this is going to be different—it is not going to be the same for me as it has been for other people. There must be some way out. This is very, very frequent. Why? Because this idea has now become too strong, there is too much force in it, and such as I am, I am unable to accept it. I am unable to live by it, unable to live with the actual acceptance of the fact that I am going to die in such and such a period of time.

I give this second picture to show you that it can happen that ideas can be too powerful, so powerful that people can no longer respond to them. Perhaps you know the saying in Hebrews "Strong meat belongeth to them that are of full age, even those who by reason of use have their senses exercised to discern both good and evil."

I think I have said enough to remind you that there can be such power in ideas that they will take hold of us and change our lives in a way that by our own decision, our own feeling of what ought to be, we ourselves are unable to do.

Now, can something similar enter into the life of man in general? We can see in the world round us that a change is needed, that the good intentions of people are not sufficient to bring about a good future for mankind. Most of us think very hard about the future. We see the danger of war and realise very well that another war would be so great a disaster that perhaps mankind would not recover from it. We see how all over the world the grasping for purely material conditions and the conception of life in terms of purely material values are making the whole economic system of the world shake and perhaps collapse. We see also great deterioration in the lives of individuals, in human relationships, in family relationships and so on. We struggle against this. We think this a terrible thing—the increasing incidence of insanity and nervous disorder, the general neurasthenia of the world, and the lack of harmony in family life. We know well enough that things must change or the future is very black, but how can change come? We must assume that it can come, otherwise it is useless to meet and talk about it.

What does it mean, to change the future? Here we have one of the elements of new ideas that are possible. Two thousand five hundred years ago, in the time of Gotama Buddha, whom I have mentioned already, there was probably for the first time clearly introduced into human thought the conception of causality and the inevitability of the causal sequence. This was a great thought, clearly formulated: "Out of *this, that* arises, and from the disappearance of *this, that* ceases to be." This thought had a very big effect because there previously had been a widespread feeling that any sort of miracle, any sort of preternatural happening was possible. The new idea was very sobering.

But, side by side with it, another idea was introduced: that escape from this general law of causality was also possible. If there was an inward change in man, he could liberate himself entirely from it. The doctrine of liberation was the essence of Gotama's teaching, and it had great power at the time, but the idea of causality later became very artificial. Within a very few generations, it was replaced by other ideas and watered down and lost sight of until it re-entered Western thought as a philosophical or scientific principle. In our Western world it has become a very important factor, because with the progress of what we call science—with our exact measurements of physical processes, our understanding or knowledge of the quantitative aspect of the exchanges of energy and so on—we see that this is a universal law.

And this has led people to think that the whole universe is just a mechanism in which everything is entirely determined. Many think that this is an inescapable conclusion—and it is indeed an inescapable conclusion if we confine ourselves to physical processes. An impartial study of the results arrived at by careful measurement and observation can allow us no doubt. When in physical science what was called the "Indeterminacy Principle" made its appearance, it looked as though there was some loophole, but this loses meaning as soon as large systems enter, and the mechanistic universe remains just as inevitable as before.

At the same time, quite untouched by these scientific conclusions, the feeling exists in man that somehow his choice is not just an illusion—he is not just a helpless spectator of things that are happening without the participation of his intention. I suppose this is not a very serious conflict for most people, and they do not feel it matters one way or another because life has to be lived just the same. It is only important in one sense: that it helps us to see the meaning of the principle that I formulated at the beginning of this lecture, that is, the principle that man is a being confronted with choice, before whom there are two different kinds of lives. Man is just a machine among machines, but a machine that can be free, can be not a machine. This would not be possible if there were not different levels of existence. On one level of existence, man is a machine living among machines; on another level of existence, there is the possibility of freedom. There are two worlds open to man—not one world far away and one here, but two worlds both here.

Just before the passage I quoted from Deuteronomy are these verses:

> For this commandment which I command thee this day, it is not hidden from thee, neither is it far off.
>
> It is not in heaven, that thou shouldest say, Who shall go up for us to heaven, and bring it unto us, that we may hear it, and do it?
>
> Neither is it beyond the sea, that thou shouldest say, Who shall go over the sea for us, and bring it unto us that we may hear it and do it?
>
> But the word is very nigh to thee, in thy mouth and in thy heart, that thou mayest do it.

This was very rightly formulated, but how can it become a powerful idea, an idea that makes people act? Only if they can be convinced of the reality of these two worlds and of the complete difference between existence in one world and existence in the other world. Is it possible that people should be convinced of such a thing? This is where I can begin to speak about Gurdjieff's ideas.

He studied and, as I will tell you in later lectures, made it one of the tasks of his life to try to understand why we live on the earth, what purpose human life serves. You might have thought that this is one of the questions that would most occupy people, but on the whole it does not occupy them very much, and because they have not thought seriously about it and found a convincing answer, they have missed a good deal that can help them to live their lives. Here I am only going to state, without explaining and certainly without trying to prove, what it is that he, Gurdjieff, conceived to be the role of man in the universe— what we exist for. He says we exist to serve a twofold purpose. The first purpose we must serve—whether we like it or not, in common with every other living being, whether animal, plant or anything else—is to serve in the transformation of energy that is required for the whole cosmic economy, particularly the economy of our solar system, our earth and our moon.

We all know that our bodies are like a chemical factory. We take in certain raw material—food and air and so on. Out of this we make the material from which our bodies are built, and also the material from which our various kinds of experience become possible. Gurdjieff adds that, in addition to this, we also produce, release and make available a certain energy required for cosmic purposes. This corresponds to what I called earlier the mechanical line, and it corresponds to what is called in the Gospel the wide gate and broad way that leads to destruction, into which many go. We are all living for the same sort of purpose as animals live—thinking, it is true, experiencing, feeling, writing books, reading books, and organizing the world and so on, but still doing it all on that level—merely being a transformation station for energy. This is one inevitable destiny that no man can escape, one purpose for which he and every other living thing were made.

But at the same time man can, while serving this purpose,

also serve another purpose, in which he can find a different destiny for himself and have a different value objectively. This can come about only if, in this process of transforming energy, he increases the efficiency or the amount of production so that he does what is necessary for him to do; he pays his debt, as it were, and has a surplus left over for himself. This is simply another way of formulating the same principle I have spoken about several times: the choice between life and death. It is the principle of the straight gate and narrow way against the broad gate and wide way, or the same principle as formulated in the words "The axe is laid at the root of the tree, and the tree that does not bear fruit is hewn down and cast into the fire." The primary purpose of the tree is firewood, and the purpose more significant to the tree and more significant objectively is to bear fruit. The same concept arises in Buddhism through "The Four Noble Truths."

From our experience, however, and from the study of history we see that, in fact, although these things have been taught in the past, they no longer have the power to affect the life of man. There are many reasons for this, but we will not consider them here. There are two extreme tendencies: One is to believe too much and too easily, the other is to believe too little. The result is that of the two possible destinies for man, people see only one and so lose the most important impulse to right action. They either say: "There is nothing more for man than this existence here, and he must make the best of it," or else they say, "He is immortal and bound in some way or another to go beyond this existence. Every individual is significant and valuable, even if he does very little about it."

On the whole, those who adopt a religious conception of man tend to take the optimistic view that all will be well providing he pays reasonable attention to certain rules, certain requirements. This is, of course, quite contrary to the teaching of all the founders of religion, whose teaching is always of the nature of "Many are called but few are chosen," but because of the tendency of people to take the rosiest view they can of a situation, this kind of severe conception of human life tends to be watered down;

and if people are unable to take the rosy view, they go to the other extreme, which also dispenses them from very serious efforts. They say, in effect, "There is nothing more in it; come, let us eat, drink and be merry, for tomorrow we die. Let us look after at least the material necessities—if not our own, at any rate the material necessities of those who are in want. This is all we can expect out of life, and all that life can expect out of us."

Between these two kinds of views, the whole future of mankind is drifting into disaster, because neither of them corresponds to reality and neither of them produces in man the one response that is essential not only for his own personal welfare, but for him to fulfill the high purpose for which he exists. The right response is that he must make efforts, struggle to raise himself above this level of mechanical existence, to lift himself out of this causal mechanism. Or, putting it in different terms, he must make for himself a soul; he must make himself an independent, free being; he must make himself, in other words, something that he is not; and he can do that only if the necessity for it appears to him with power, with force.

I have quoted from Mosaic, Buddhist and Christian sacred books, and I could have quoted also from the Upanishads, from the Koran or from the writings of saints and mystics of all ages. I could have shown you how the doctrine of choice between life and death, between the supremely valuable and the worthless, runs like a golden thread through them all. Hearing me, you may well be tempted to ask what need there is, then, of a new world. Should not our aim be rather to restore what has been well understood and powerful in men's lives in the past, rather than seek for a new teacher and a new gospel? In one sense, it is true—and Gurdjieff himself always emphasized it in his teaching and in his writing—that the truth about human destiny has been understood and the way of life followed far better in the past than in our time.

I think that I have said enough to make the answer clear. What we lack is not the idea in the sense of knowledge of what should be done, but the *Idea* in the sense of the living force that makes that knowledge effective in our actions. Those of us who have studied Gurdjieff's teaching have felt in it, above all, the force that drives to action and the sense of urgency that makes it possible to pay the price without waiting till tomorrow.

It is very difficult for people brought up in the environment of Western thought to experience the true sense of choice between life and death that presents itself to man. We are professedly Christian peoples, and the teachings of Jesus Christ, as preserved for us in the Gospels, states the choice without compromise. But Christianity as we know it is not the teaching of Jesus Christ but the distorted remnants that have survived the falsifications of Greece and the power politics of Rome. Gurdjieff adds in his discussion of Christianity the further baneful influence of what he calls the "Babylonian dualism," expressed in the doctrine of "heaven" and "hell." This idea for a time had great power over the minds of men, but it does not correspond to reality, and it has long ceased to be a dominating factor in human behavior.

The power of Gurdjieff's teaching lies in the elimination of everything fictitious and the return to the naked reality of human destiny. The choice between life and death is not a matter of another life in which we only half believe. It is the ever-present situation of every moment in the life of man. It is the choice between misery and rejoicing, between the immediate experience of life and the emptiness of no experience at all. It is the choice between helplessness and strength. When we turn our attention outwards towards the suffering and bewilderment of mankind, it is the choice between the sense of frustration and the confidence that something effectual can be done. In contemplating our own personal destiny, it is the choice between the doubt whether our life has any meaning and the certainty that in the scheme of things we have a necessary part to play. In the face of death, it is the choice between the terror of a wasted life that cannot be redeemed, and the peace and satisfaction of him who quits the scene with his debts paid and his duty done.

On what does all this turn? What is the real meaning of this choice? These questions can be answered only if we understand Gurdjieff's teaching about the actual and the *potential* nature of man. We exaggerate to the point of absurdity the value and the powers of man, such as he is, and we underestimate and misconceive the almost unlimited possibilities of achievement for the man who follows the path of self-creation.

The starting point of Gurdjieff's teaching is that man as we know him is a machine, controlled by external influences. He has no power of effective action. Nothing in his life is determined by his own will and choice. This is an assertion very difficult to accept, and for many it is the greatest obstacle in the way of approach to Gurdjieff's teaching. We are so thoroughly saturated with the notion of our ability, within limits, to do what we decide, that the assertion of our complete helplessness seems either ridiculous or disheartening. Nevertheless, it is true and can be established by each one of us beyond all doubt if we are prepared to observe impartially our own behaviour, or simply take into account the well-known facts of the working of the human nervous system and the chemistry of the human body. Our nervous system is a mechanism that reacts to external influences just as a typewriter types when the keys are worked. Many of you have no doubt read Sir Charles Sherrington's *Rede* Lecture on the "Integrative Action of the Nervous System" and will remember how he compares the mechanism of our behaviour to a lock that is fitted by the nervous system like a key; and if we ask the question "What turns this key?" he answers, "The external world."

There is nothing in man as we know him which is capable of independent, self-determined action. That is the picture of the "man machine," as Gurdjieff calls him, and before we can understand anything objectively about human nature and human destiny, we have first to recognize that this is a true picture. A strange situation exists today. It is widely said, especially by scientists and medical men, that man is a machine in the sense I have just described, and yet the very people who make this assertion entertain prejudices, make demands, and themselves behave as though they and all other men were free beings, responsible for their actions. They criticize and judge other people, and even become indignant over behaviour that, according to their own theory, is not the result of any intention and could not be otherwise than it is.

It is no easy task to convince oneself or to convince others that men are machines, and yet this simple truth provides the only possible explanation of human behaviour as we observe it, whether individually or in the masses. As we survey the life of man, we must see that it cannot be accounted for in terms of intentional, voluntary action. People do what they never intended, and what they intend, they do not do. This applies just as much to those who are called strong, successful people as to unsuccessful, weak people.

When man first sees the reality of this situation face to face, he can scarcely escape from a feeling of terror as he looks forward into his own future. He sees that his life must of necessity be determined by the combination of external circumstances that chance or fate will bring. He is bound to drift helplessly through the stream of events in which he is immersed. If the stream threatens to bear him to destruction, he has no power to escape from it. Then and then only can the idea of self-creation begin to have power over him. He dare not remain such as he is.

In what I have just been saying, I have presented Gurdjieff's teaching in terms of this life only. I did so because we have in this life all the evidence that is needed to demonstrate that it is disastrous madness to neglect the work of self-creation. Gurdjieff's teaching is not, however, confined to the experience of this life only. The choice between life and death takes its sharpest and most urgent expression in contemplating the cessation of our own existence. It is true that all principles of self-creation would apply, even if the prospect that we contemplate stops short with our old age and our death. Gurdjieff asserts, on the basis of evidence of which I shall say a little in the later lectures, that the man who does not work for the creation of his own *being* has, and can have, no life but this; but the man who works and struggles for his own perfection has latent powers that are not confined to this visible life. When we go beyond the visible, facts in the ordinary sense are lacking. Facts there are, but they are all of such a nature that they cannot be established by pro-

cesses in this mechanical level of existence. People who imagine
that facts can be established in this mechanical level (e.g., in the
so-called evidence of spiritualism), just do not see the alternative
explanation.

At the same time, facts can be established, but only on a different level of existence and a different level of experience. This
I cannot either ask you to accept nor can I explain it in any detail. I am adding it only for completeness of the picture, because
sooner or late, there has to re-enter effectively into the life of
man the idea that he is born with the *possibility* of living after
death, not with the *guarantee* of it. He is born with the possibility of survival and of a very great degree of further progress and
of serving a very high purpose—providing he makes use of this
possibility that exists in his life: the possibility of producing by
his own efforts a surplus of the energy that in any case is required of him. Whether he likes it or not, he has to restore the
talent that was given to him, but if he will work and make something in addition, not only can he have something for himself,
but be of different value not only to his fellow men, but also to
higher purposes. This is a fundamental conception. Let us see if
I can put it succinctly.

Gurdjieff taught that man is a being with two destinies: one
unavoidable; the other that it is in his power to have, but only if
he himself earns it. And this second destiny, both as regards this
life and any possibilities of another life, is incomparably more
valuable than the first. As things are in the world at the present
time, a very small proportion of people are doing anything effective for the attainment of the second destiny.

This has certain very bad consequences, because the amount
of this energy or matter that has to be produced in the life of
man is determined not by himself, but by general influences.
Suppose that we had a flock of sheep and required so much
wool. If the sheep began to produce less wool, we should have
to increase our flock. The population of the world is increased
in very much the same way as the number of sheep that have to
be kept as the wool deteriorates in quality and quantity, and this
carries with it very unsatisfactory consequences for mankind.

If what I have been saying is right—if it is, in fact, important to us individually and important to our race as a whole and to higher purposes also that a sufficiently large number of people should struggle for the attainment of the second destiny, for living in the second world—then how is the necessity for this to be more widely felt? If it can be more widely felt, then future generations will enter into a new world. If not, they will not even keep the old world that we have known. It is about the answer to that question that I am going to speak in the next three lectures.

It may help you to understand something of the significance of these ideas for the future of mankind, if we try to visualize the effect on human relationships of a widespread realization that a man who does not struggle to attain a high destiny is no more than an animal and, indeed, to be despised, which an animal is not. This is as far removed as possible from current ways of looking at people. They are valued for what they have—whether personal attractions or material possessions—for the position they occupy in life, and for similar factors that may have no connection at all with any true value.

If once it is understood that the one true criterion that objectively decides the value of a man is his ability to struggle with himself, then only those would be respected who showed by their lives that they had achieved some measure of success in this direction. Their advice and help would be sought after, as people who had to some extent freed themselves from the mechanicalness of ordinary existence, from slavery to external things, from inner weakness. Ambition, the desire for power, fame and admiration, and the other motives that lead people to work and strive for positions of authority would be seen as defects and weaknesses unworthy of a true man. The world would seek for teachers rather than rulers, for those who could set an example rather than those who dominate and impress. The idea of a ruler who is himself the helpless slave of his own passions and his own automatism would be seen for what it is: a ludicrous travesty of a true master of men.

A further inevitable consequence would be the disappearance

of the mutual misvaluation among different castes or classes and between nations and races. Such misvaluation is only possible so long as artificial values dominate the mind of man. Wars of aggression and conquest, ideological and religious wars, all have their origin in false conceptions of what is important for man. It will be by no means obvious to you if I say that only an understanding of the twofold destiny of man can put an end to war. I propose, therefore, to finish this lecture by saying a little about Gurdjieff's teaching on the subject of war, its origin and the possibility of its ceasing.

Our attitude towards war is altogether false. We tend, as a matter of course, to regard war as the result of the intentional action of some wicked man or group of men or of some nation with a lust for conquest and power. Wars appear, to both sides engaged in them, as defense against some aggression or as necessary for the furthering of some worthy or even sacred cause. Even those who most detest war and are prepared to sacrifice their liberty, or even their lives, to save themselves from becoming involved in it, conceive it as a wicked action, deliberately undertaken.

In reality, war is not like this at all. It is a terrible madness that overtakes mankind, when people lose even the little sense of reality they usually have. War is the supreme manifestation of human helplessness. This applies to all forms of mutual destruction, whether revolution and civil war within a nation or armed conflict between nations and the peoples of the world.

War has a twofold origin. The first is outside of man and arises independently. The second is within man and is due to his own weakness and failure. From time to time a special state of tension arises on the earth, which Gurdjieff calls the state of "Solioonensius." This state of tension arises from the relations between the planets. I do not mean by this that it is something supernatural or mysterious. It is a perfectly natural process, connected with the changes in the balance of electrical and other energy in the solar system. For example, it is already suspected by science that the occurrence of sunspots has an effect upon the human psyche.

It may help you to understand what I mean by calling Solioo-nensius a perfectly natural process if you consider a simple phe-nomenon, well-known to all. I refer to the effect in Great Britain of the east wind, or in the Mediterranean of the sirocco. When the east wind blows, people become irritable and nothing seems to go right. I once became interested in this because I wanted to see whether it was a real or an imaginary effect. I asked a num-ber of people to observe carefully and let me know as objective-ly as possible whether they could detect a state of inner tension caused by the east wind. Nearly everyone confirmed that a state of irritability did, in fact, arise in them even before they were aware that the east wind was blowing.

In a more subtle and pervasive manner, great regions of the earth's surface, and sometimes even the whole of the earth, be-come subject to a state of tension that produces in people a strong sense of dissatisfaction with their conditions of life. They become irritable or aggressive, apprehensive, nervous and high-ly suggestible. Gurdjieff said that knowledge of Solioonensius existed thousands of years ago, and that he took the term from a very ancient tradition. At the present time, its significance has been forgotten or lost.

The point is that there are two completely different ways in which people can react to a state of Solioonensius. It always arouses dissatisfaction, but this may be external or internal. Ex-ternal dissatisfaction leads to external conflict; internal dissatis-faction strengthens the desire to struggle with oneself. Those who understand the necessity for working on themselves and achieving the second destiny find in that state of tension the greatest possibility of incentive and force to make them work harder. But those who do not have this feeling, this realization, project outwards their dissatisfaction and become hostile and an-gry with other people—suspicious, jealous and the rest of it—and then, defenseless against these mass psychoses, begin to hate. And the very people who, only a few years before, could not conceive of themselves consenting to the idea of war be-come involved in the destruction of other people. And those other people, passing through the same mass psychosis with the same justification, wish in turn to destroy their existence.

It is possible by careful study of history and of various psychological processes to verify this. And once you understand it, you will see that there is no way by which war can be stopped other than by making people understand the necessity for this work. Otherwise, they have no defense against this state of tension; no contrivances, no organization, no good resolutions can avail, because there is a physio-chemical process involved. This state of tension must produce the result. We do not know when such a state of tension will come over the world again. When it is absent, we do not feel war as something possible, but when it approaches, nothing can be done unless an idea can come into the world that can act on a sufficiently large number of people to enable them to turn this force in a different direction.

This is one reason why the change—the transition period—from one epoch to another, from one world to another, is a dangerous period. Old ideas have lost their momentum and can no longer move the world. New ideas have not yet gained momentum. All through history, and even before the beginning of history, we find such periods accompanied by war and revolution, not because war and revolution are inevitable in themselves but because people have lacked that discrimination that would enable them to use this situation rightly. If we are able to go into a world in which this is understood, then the course of history can be different, because the destiny of all mankind can be raised to a higher level. There is no higher purpose in the life of man than to bring about this great transition.

If a new world is to come, we must first create it in ourselves. You may ask how the work of a few people can change the world. It has always been so. *Ideas* are powerful, not organizations. Nothing can be done by outward force; everything can be done by inner strength.

Let me try to give you a picture of how such changes can come. Some of you no doubt are cooks and have had to make sauces. Suppose I am making some sauce, like a hollandaise, that is liable to demulsify, that is, the butter separates from the egg. This can be a terrifying experience if you are making a sauce for 60 or 70 people with pounds of butter and dozens of eggs. An inexperienced cook loses his head and beats the sauce violently—but only makes things worse. A good cook pours a little water at one edge of the bowl and stirs quietly until it turns back again, and then it spreads through the whole mass until the sauce is right again.

The first time you do this, it seems almost miraculous. It is the same with the world. Everywhere people are stirring violently to get oil and water to mix. This cannot happen. The part of wisdom is to establish here and there centers in which right relationships can exist by the power of a common understanding of what is ultimately important. From such centers there can spread throughout the world—perhaps far more quickly than you might imagine possible—the seeds of a new world.

I have said nothing yet about Gurdjieff himself. Next, I will speak about his life and work. You may have understood from what I have said why I am convinced that in his teaching we have the seeds of a new world. Even so, I should not leave you to infer but should say clearly why it is that, according to my understanding, his teaching has such a unique significance. No teaching can be divorced from the teacher. Abstract, impersonal ideas, can never have power. If Gurdjieff in his life had not exemplified his own teaching, and if he had not shown that it is possible to go by the way he had revealed, his teaching, however convincing to the mind and however powerful in its emotional appeal, would have lacked the one essential element that can give force to an idea. A world on the brink of disaster, unable to believe and not daring to hope, has need above all of a guide who with confidence will give a lead and show a way that he is himself prepared to take. Gurdjieff has died, leaving the world the example of a life lived without compromise in terms of the ideas that are his legacy to the world.

O

"WITH THE DISPERSAL of the 'Seekers of the Truth,' Gurdjieff conceived it to be his own task to make known to the world the knowledge they had discovered."

Chapter 2

Gurdjieff—The Man and His Work

MY TASK NOW IS TO GIVE YOU some account of Gurdjieff's life and work. My sources of information are in part his own autobiographical writing and in part what I heard from him personally in conversation. For the story of his last 30 years I have been able, to some small extent, to draw on my own personal experience.

To start with, I must try to give you some picture of Gurdjieff's own country, that is, the Southern Caucasus. It is not easy for one who has not lived in the Near and Middle East to form a picture of the extraordinary mingling of races, religions and cultures—some very ancient, some relatively modern—that makes the Caucasus region almost unique on the earth. Waves of civilization have reached the Caucasus from North, South, East and West. It is like the high-water mark on the seashore left by the tide, where children playing at collecting shells and seaweed know that they will find the strangest treasures. West European, Slavonic, Turkish, Roman, Greek, Central Asian, Persian, Hittite, Babylonian and Sumerian cultures, together with others so ancient that their origin is unknown, have in turn swept up to the Caucasus and then receded, leaving behind them living remains thar have persisted to the present day. Not only this, but the collapse of civilizations has also been followed by migrations of people from the great rivers—the Tigris and the Euphrates, the Volga and the

Oxus—which have further enriched the Caucasus with the traditions of ancient centers of culture. We have nothing in Europe comparable to this region, where dozens of races speaking many languages, some almost unknown, preserve the remains of former cultures and old customs that carry one back into the distant past of the human race.

Gurdjieff was born in Alexandropol near the Persian frontier of Russia on December 28, 1877.* His own family came from the Ionian Greeks of Caesarea, who have a continuous history dating back before the Christian era. The Greeks of Caesarea have preserved their culture through centuries of foreign rule, and they have a spirit of independence that aroused the admiration of all those who saw them, as I did, after the exchange of populations between Greece and Turkey in 1925. In the 16th century, some of the Greek families of Caesarea withdrew towards the northeast after the overthrow of the Byzantine Empire, and among them were Gurdjieff's ancestors. They were what we should now call ranchers, that is, owners of great herds of sheep and cattle. In the middle of the last century they left Turkey for the Russian Caucasus.

After the Russo-Turkish War of 1877, his father, who had lost his herds through an epidemic of cattle disease, established himself as a carpenter in Kars, which was then an important Russian military center near the Turkish frontier. In Kars entered one of the great influences of Gurdjieff's early life, when a saintly man, Father Borsch, dean of the Military Cathedral, who had known him as a young chorister, offered to make himself responsible for the boy's education. Gurdjieff was taught by priests and doctors, in accordance with his father's plan that he should prepare himself for what he and the dean conceived as a single vocation: to be physician for the body and confessor for the soul.

The boy himself was interested in mechanics and in natural and medical science—above all, in psychoneurology. He also delighted in the acquisition of skill in every kind of manual trade. Nevertheless, the strange environment of the Caucasus, combined with several unusual experiences that pointed to the exis-

* [See footnote on page 6.]

tence of supernatural forces in the life of man, turned his mind towards the conflict between the materialism of Western science, which he valued for its methods of accurate observation and measurement, and the evidence of phenomena of which science was powerless to give an account. He was also steeped in the old traditions preserved in the ballads and sagas of the Asiatic bards. His father was himself a bard, famed for his knowledge of the legends of the ancient Assyrian and Sumerian cultures. In later life, Gurdjieff was deeply impressed by the discovery of cuneiform inscriptions that showed the accuracy with which these poems had been preserved through thousands of years.

He began on his own to visit the ruins of ancient cities and made archaeological discoveries that convinced him that in some former epoch mankind had possessed knowledge, since lost, of the true sense and purpose of human life and the way to its fulfillment. He resolved to devote himself to the search for the reality underlying the seeming contradictions in the facts he had encountered. He could find no solution in Western science and philosophy or in the teaching of any of the Christian Churches or Moslem sects with which he had come in contact. Nevertheless, evidence accumulated that the knowledge and the way he was seeking might have been preserved in isolated communities. He made up his mind to travel and search until he should find the truth for himself.

Barely grown to manhood, he collected round him a handful of young men inspired with the same convictions and hopes. Together they formed a small society that styled itself the "Seekers of Truth." Singly or in twos and threes, they succeeded in visiting the countries where they hoped to find traces of real knowledge. In the course of their journeys, they met a number of remarkable men who joined them in their search and, with their experience and material resources, greatly extended the scope of their enquiry. Their travels took them far into Africa, through Persia, Turkestan, Tibet, India and the Far East, the Indonesian Archipelago and even as far as Australia. They also travelled in little-known parts of Europe, visiting monasteries and other places where ancient traditions might be preserved. Their travels were from time to time interrupted to enable them to take stock of what each had found. They kept abreast of the progress of Western science, particularly astronomy, chemistry, medicine and psychology.

Gurdjieff tells us in his writings that, as time went on, he became more and more engrossed by what he calls the "*idée fixé* of his inner world"—namely, the need to understand the sense and significance of human existence. Man, as he saw it, must by his existence serve a Great Purpose, and this purpose must equally be served by all. He was convinced that Western philosophy was very far from understanding this Great Purpose—but he found the popular theories current in the East equally unsatisfying.

The thirst for an understanding of this central problem of human life was shared by the other members of the Seekers of Truth. As time went on, they found it possible to penetrate to places quite inaccessible to the ordinary traveller. They met many extraordinary men—sometimes individual dervishes or monks, sometimes whole brotherhoods or communities—possessing in varying degrees insight into the nature of man and the secrets of human destiny. They were shown practical methods, transmitted from remote antiquity, for the development of the latent powers of man.

The journeys of the Seekers of Truth came to an end before 1908. Some of them joined and remained in one or other of the brotherhoods they had succeeded in reaching, others died. They had found personal guidance and help in their own search for an understanding of the meaning and purpose of their own existence. But they had also accumulated data that showed the force of the ancient traditions and the extent to which the fundamental problems of man and the universe had been understood in the remote past. Having at the same time an intimate knowledge of Western traditions and modern science, they were able to weld them all together into a single system of ideas. There is no doubt that in this work Gurdjieff was the leading spirit and driving force.

Before ending my account of this period of Gurdjieff's life, I must refer to strange and persistent personal misfortunes that seem to have formed an integral part of his destiny. To an unusual extent his life was, again and again, endangered by accident and disease. No traveller entering into close contact with the populations of Eastern cities or with the insect-ridden valleys of Asia, from the Maeander to the Yangtze, can hope to avoid infection. Gurdjieff contracted nearly all the diseases of the East. These, he has said, left their permanent marks on his bodily organism. He has also described how three times he was almost killed by accidental bullet wounds in the early skirmishes in some war, first in Crete, then in Tibet and the third time in the Caucasus in the fighting between Cossacks and Gurians. Later, automobiles took the place of bullets, and he was several times nearly killed in motor-car accidents. His life was always an alternation of intensive activity with enforced stoppages due to accident and illness. No one who met him can doubt that his immense force was derived, in part at least, from his almost unceasing struggle with bodily suffering.

With the dispersal of the Seekers of Truth, Gurdjieff conceived it to be his own task to make known to the world the knowledge they had discovered. He had come more and more to realize the helplessness of modern man, having become the plaything of forces he had invoked but could in no way control. He saw this helplessness as universal, pervading equally the East and the West. But against this he could set his own conviction that the world could be saved from a terrible succession of disastrous wars and revolutions, of economic and social catastrophes, if only the right understanding of human destiny could again be introduced into the life of man.

He realized that to carry through such a task many helpers and much money would be needed. He set himself, for the first time in his life, the primary aim of accumulating wealth. He engaged in commerce and finance—public works, contracting, buying and selling of businesses and development of oil fields. He also applied his immense knowledge of the human organism to the cure of drug addicts and dipsomaniacs, often being paid very large sums by rich families to undertake an apparently hopeless case.

I should refer here to his extraordinary powers of work. At several periods in his life he worked for months with only two or three hours sleep each day. This he did even when in bad health or when not fully recovered from an accident. No one who associated with him in one of these periods of furious activity could understand how he was able to produce such personal energy for himself and such driving force behind others.

By 1912 he was by all standards a rich man, and his work had become known in many circles. He decided to lose no more time but to found in Moscow an organization that he called the "Institute for the Harmonious Development of Man According to the Ideas of G. Gurdjieff." He started work with several groups of students, each specializing in one aspect of the work he wished to undertake. Some were engaged in psychological work, others in the study of the plastic arts and music. He also devoted particular attention to medicine and the chemistry of the human body. For these activities, he purchased and equipped a large estate near Moscow. He had recently married a Polish lady of the well-known Ostrovsky family, and they decided to make their home in Russia.

Then came the First World War. Despite increasing difficulties, he continued his work in Moscow and even extended it to St. Petersburg, but he concentrated more upon psychological work than upon scientific experiments. In 1915, he was joined by a very remarkable man, the famous Russian philosopher and writer P.D. Ouspensky, who became his pupil and took an active part in the organization of his work. I need not speak in detail of the years between 1915 and 1920. Ouspensky's own book *In Search of the Miraculous** gives a dramatic account of that period when Tsarist Russia was destroyed forever. A small but devoted circle of his Russian pupils continued their work with Gurdjieff to preserve for the world, through that time of chaos, what he himself had learned.

In 1918, he withdrew to the Northern Caucasus and undertook intensive practical teaching with a number of pupils who had succeeded in following him from Moscow and St. Petersburg.

* New York: Harcourt, Brace & Company, Inc., 1949.

Civil war soon made life there impossible, and he undertook a hazardous journey through uninhabited regions of the Caucasus mountains and finally reached Tiflis, the capital of Georgia. The then government of Georgia was favorable to his work and gave him facilities for re-establishing his Institute in Tiflis. Here, new pupils came to him of diverse nationalities. He began to elaborate his teaching of the sacred dances and rhythmical exercises that he had studied in Central Asia and the Far East. He had long before gained in Asia the reputation of being the greatest living authority on temple dances, some of which he had studied in monasteries and temples difficult of access, where they were used for developing the spiritual powers of man.

In 1920, the tide of war and revolution flooded the Southern Caucasus. With great difficulty Gurdjieff extricated himself and many of his pupils. He came to Constantinople, where I met him for the first time.

My first meeting with Gurdjieff was in the Palace of Kuru Chesme, the home of the Prince Sabaheddin, nephew of the Turkish Sultan, himself a profound student, who had told me that I was to meet the most remarkable man he had ever known. My first impressions of Gurdjieff were of the purity of his Turkish accent, rare for a Greek, and of his extraordinary knowledge of hypnotism, in which Sabaheddin and I were at that time greatly interested. His appearance was so striking that for many years I did not realize that he was of only moderate stature. When he took off the *kalpak* he was wearing, his magnificent head, completely shaven, produced a strange sense of harmony with sweeping black moustaches, strong eyebrows and eyes that at first seemed jet black. When he smiled, his whole appearance changed— even his eyes became light and transparent. I could not help feeling that I had met someone out of the ordinary run of men.

I learned that Ouspensky was independently giving lectures in Constantinople. Thomas de Hartmann, the Russian composer who had been working with Gurdjieff on the music for his dances, and Alexander de Salzmann, the famous stage designer, had begun to develop their own particular lines as part of his general

* New York: Alfred Knopf, Inc., 1922.

plan. Gurdjieff evidently did not intend to settle permanently in Constantinople and asked me to help him get to Europe.

In the meantime, Ouspensky's book *Tertium Organum** had appeared in England and America, where it attracted considerable attention. Lady Rothermere had taken a keen interest in Ouspensky, and a succession of telegrams arrived inviting him to London. Ouspensky decided to go to London alone. Gurdjieff remained some time longer in Turkey. He finally went to Berlin, preferring it to Western Europe because he always hoped to reopen the path to Russia, where many of his pupils had remained.

Conditions in Germany made work there impossible, and in the autumn of 1922 he finally settled in France. He bought the Château du Prieuré at Fontainebleau, and again started the Institute for the Harmonious Development of Man, with a nucleus of his older pupils from Tiflis and Constantinople. Many English people came to the Institute—either permanently or as visitors— mostly pupils of Ouspensky, who since the end of 1921 had been lecturing in London on Gurdjieff's system.

Very intensive work began. Gurdjieff planned demonstrations of his dances and exercises in Europe and the United States. His considerable material resources, accumulated before the war, had been dissipated in the course of travels made under such difficult and arduous conditions. It was indeed only possible to keep the Institute going because all those living at the Prieuré were prepared to work without respite on the farm and in the house on very meager rations. These very circumstances were converted by Gurdjieff into conditions for inner work, and no one who spent even a week or two at the Prieuré between 1922 and 1924 can forget the intensity of that particular period.

For me personally, my stay at the Prieuré in the summer of 1923 was the start of a new life. From personal experience I became convinced that what I had so far regarded as theoretically possible for man could be realized in practice for myself, if I were prepared to work.

I was more than ever impressed by Gurdjieff's amazing versatility. While I was there, he was building a Russian steam bath, quarried out of the Fontainebleau rocks. No one could handle pickaxe and crowbar as he could. He was equally at home with the animals or repairing the power plant. He was a marvelous cook. But it was, above all, in the "Study House," a building of unusual design improvised from an astonishing variety of materials, that we saw the most striking demonstration of his powers. It was there that he worked out all the new and complicated dances that he was then teaching, showing each executant exactly how the movements should be made.

The theoretical explanations of cosmological and psychological questions—the development of the rich symbolism described in Ouspensky's *In Search of the Miraculous*—gave place at this time to a severely practical approach in which physical efforts played a large part. This, of course, had already started in the Caucasus, but there was now a new element, the germ of an objective that was beginning to take shape in our minds: the task to be accomplished of making his teaching known to the world.

His own time was divided between earning money and driving forward the work of the Institute. Finding himself in a strange country whose language even was quite unfamiliar, he could not engage in commerce with the same ease as in Russia or the Caucasus. He was thus thrown back on his knowledge of medicine and psychology. He undertook the cure of drug addicts and drunkards. By this most difficult and exhausting work—for which he had already long before been famous in Central Asia— he was able to earn the money required to keep the Institute going. I have myself seen the seemingly impossible cases he undertook and the almost-miraculous results achieved. But the strain on his physique was too great and debts were accumulating, so he decided to go to America before completing his preparations.

He went in 1925, taking with him some 40 people to give demonstrations of sacred dances and "movements," to give lectures and to meet a number of important Americans who had expressed the wish to know more of his ideas. The visit, which lasted only six weeks, was a success. He planned to return again in the fall to found in the United States and other countries branches of the main institute in France. He left behind a well-known English journalist, A.R. Orage, the editor of the *New Age* and the

New English Weekly, who made himself responsible for the pre-paratory work.

Ouspensky had separated from Gurdjieff in 1925 and was teaching in London in isolation from the other groups of Gurd-jieff's pupils. In this again, I think we must see an example of Gurdjieff's experimentation and testing. He more than once brought about a separation between himself and his most valued pupils—perhaps in order to see for himself how his ideas would affect the lives of people out of contact with his personal teach-ing.

Within a few weeks of Gurdjieff's return from America, he was all but killed in an automobile accident, as a result of which he lost his memory for months and only very gradually recovered. From a profoundly moving passage written by him about that time, we know of his realization that there was then only a limit-ed time available for the accomplishment of his task. He resolved to put his ideas into the form of a written exposition, so com-posed as to lead people step by step to an understanding of prac-tical work upon themselves. The next 10 years were entirely de-voted to writing, and he withdrew wholly from contact with the outside world, except for necessary business matters.

It is indispensable to refer to the general course of Gurdjieff's life during this period. While writing, he displayed an intensity of concentration that at times completely isolated him from his sur-roundings. Sometimes he worked continuously day and night at the Prieuré. At other times he travelled, usually by car, in France and other European countries. Then he would often stop his car by the side of the road and write for hours on a stone or in a wayside café. Much of his work was done at the Café de la Paix in Paris, where, amidst the bustle and confusion of the life around him, he would write all day and late into the night. No one could speak to him, however urgent the occasion, until he turned his attention to them of his own accord.

He wrote mostly in Russian. The manuscript was translated into English, French and German, each version being constantly reread to him for correction. Those who participated in this work have described it as unlike any ordinary experience.

In order to have even an approximate conception of the work undertaken by Gurdjieff between 1927 and 1948, it would be necessary to read and study the third series of his writings, which has been accessible only to students who have already worked on the first and second series. His work was partly concerned with his own inner world, partly with the needs of his worn-out body, and partly with the what he calls "obscure but all-important factors in the human psyche." It is this latter motive that is hard to understand for anyone who imagines that the modern European or American is a normal, *balanced* human being. On the contrary, all with few exceptions are unbalanced people who have quite lost contact with reality and who, therefore, it is very difficult to help towards a normal sane existence.

Gurdjieff came more and more clearly to see that the ways of helping people that have been used in the past are no longer applicable—because modern man cannot even listen to what is most necessary for him to hear. Notwithstanding so many years of profound study of the human psyche, Gurdjieff reached the conclusion as late as 1927 that a new and more penetrating approach to the problem must be undertaken. He accordingly imposed on himself a way of life that would, as he says, "cause each person to take off the mask kindly provided by their papa and mama" and disclose the depths of his or her nature. The procedure adopted he describes as "finding the most sensitive corn of each person, from whatever class or race he might come and whatever position he might hold, and treading on it rather violently." It can well be imagined that such a procedure made him many new enemies and even scandalized many old friends. Since he carried his procedure into every kind of relationship, it is not surprising that stories of a most damaging nature should have begun to spread at his expense.

Very few people were able to see the necessity or even the sense of his actions, and there is no question that many obstacles were created to the acceptance of his teaching. Nevertheless, for anyone who has felt the obscurity of the human psyche, it is obvious that what he did was indispensable—partly to establish the facts that it was necessary to know and partly also for the further aim—equally important and necessary—of trying to recover his own health. Not only was his bodily strength almost destroyed by the automobile accident, but he carried the results of many serious diseases contracted in the course of his travels in different parts of the world.

In 1931 he again visited New York, and before the outbreak of the Second World War he paid several further visits to America. The Prieuré was finally closed down in 1932, and in 1934 he settled in Paris. He was there when war broke out, and he remained throughout the German occupation. In spite of all difficulties, he continued and even started new work with his French pupils. He held them together, teaching them new methods appropriate to the conditions in which they were living. His manuscripts were constantly being read in his presence and revised, in order to bring to perfection the exposition of his ideas.

The period from 1939 to 1948 was one of the utmost difficulty and privation for himself and his work. Those who were directly in contact with him were fewer in number than in the past, while those who misunderstood his ideas and mistrusted his methods had increased. Very much misunderstanding existed. Only a few who knew him well and had worked closely with him had some understanding of his aim. But the three series of writings had been prepared and were available when a propitious moment for their publication should arrive. They were being studied in manuscript form in various parts of the world by small groups of his former pupils. All was ready. The seeds sown during the previous 50 years had grown to maturity. Externally at its lowest ebb, his work had reached an inner intensity greater than ever before. Through what channels was this force to be released?

In 1948 he began to let it be known that the time had come for a new phase of work. He had completed some time before this the testing of the methods that he had worked out, proving their suitability for our abnormal conditions of life and for the peculiar psyche of Western people. He also judged that there would be sufficient time before a fresh onset of tension in the world for these ideas to spread. If they were able to spread widely enough and rapidly enough, they might perhaps so change people's understanding that if such a state of tension were to again arise, the forces released should direct themselves into positive rather than destructive channels.

So it came about that in the summer of 1948, many people who had not seen each other for many years and others who had never met at all began to arrive in Paris and went round to see him in his little flat, re-establishing contact first with him and then with one another. Everything seemed to be going normally, as if work with him would continue as before, when again there was one of these automobile accidents that, with bullet wounds and disease, make a terrifying pattern in his life. Once again, by all ordinary standards, he should have been killed. My wife and I were with him in Paris at that time. He was driving down to Cannes, and we were to follow him down the next day. He returned in an ambulance, and I had perhaps the most extraordinary experience of my life when I saw with my own eyes the power he had over his own body. He was terribly injured by this accident, which should have killed any man, let alone a man over 70, but he very quickly recovered.

It seems to me that, in some way connected with this accident, a decision was taken that he could at last go forward with his plans for the dissemination of his ideas. Soon after this accident, he took the decision that he would publish the first series of his writing, and he charged some of his older pupils to undertake the arrangements for printing. Four translations were taken to America, Great Britain, Germany and France. Translations into Russian and Spanish were to follow. Having selected the United States as the first country in which his books should appear, he made a private visit to New York in December 1948. He remained until the end of January, by which time he had completed the arrangements with Harcourt, Brace and World for the publication of his own book and also of Ouspensky's book *In Search of the Miraculous.*

He spent his 72nd birthday in New York and, I have a vivid memory of him surrounded by his old pupils with many of their children sitting at his feet. His moustaches were now white, but his head was still clean-shaven and his complexion as fresh as when I had first met him nearly 30 years before. His smile came more frequently and conveyed an overwhelming compassion and goodness. To those of us who heard him speak to the pupils who came to see him from many parts of America, it was clear that a great step forward was being prepared.

He returned to Paris and intensified his work. Pupils began almost daily to arrive from France and other countries to visit him at his little flat in the center of Paris. Many hundreds received personal help and guidance from him in the course of the year. He simplified and concentrated his message ever more and more: *Only by the unremitting struggle of the individual for his self-perfecting can a force be created that will change the world.*

Driving himself, as always, unmercifully, he alarmed those of us who were in close touch with him, lest his physical strength should prove unequal to the demands he was making upon himself. He attached the utmost importance to the early appearance of his book in America and would himself have sailed to New York on October 20th to give it his final personal direction.

But the end came suddenly. He died in the American Hospital in Paris on October 29th. There his body lay for four days, visited by hundred of his pupils including many who had flown over from the United States, England and other countries. His funeral was a moving demonstration of the love and trust that he had inspired in those who knew him. The Russian Cathedral in Paris was crowded. There were his own pupils from France and from countries overseas, side by side with hundreds of Parisians from every walk of life who knew him as philanthropist and good friend of those in need of help. The funeral oration pronounced by the Russian archimandrite was a noble tribute to a deeply religious man who had long ceased to be associated with any one church or any one creed.

Gurdjieff's teaching is in his writings. They are his final message to his fellow men. Those of us who have studied with him for many years are convinced that his teaching corresponds to the needs of a world that is passing through a momentous transition. We want, in these days above all, to learn how to live, to know both what we ought to do and also how to do it. This is what Gurdjieff has taught us. He leaves the scene at the moment when his work is done. His writings are far more than a fitting memorial of a great life—they are the material for a new world.

○

REMEMBER you come here
having already understood the
necessity of struggling with
yourself—only with yourself.
Therefore thank everyone who
gives you the opportunity.

—An aphorism inscribed in a special script
above the walls of the Study House at
Gurdjieff's Institute for the Harmonious
Development of Man, Château du Prieuré,
near Fontainebleau, France.

Chapter 3

"Work on Oneself"

THROUGH AND THROUGH, Gurdjieff's teaching is practical. It is concerned with the concrete situation of our immediate existence and what we make of it. This is equally true whether it is on the scale of the momentary choice of "yes" or "no," or whether it shows us how to find our own answer to the ultimate question "What is my significance in the universe?" But because we are so subjective and so full of illusion, we cannot even begin to understand concrete reality, either within ourselves or outside, without preparation. We cannot even come to the idea of "work on ourselves" without preparation. Gurdjieff cannot speak to people with no sense of reality—only to those who already have some degree of understanding. Therefore, before I can begin to describe his methods of work, I must say something about preparation.

The first task is clarification of one's own aim. This everyone has to do for himself. I cannot borrow or steal an aim from someone else. I have to decide for myself what is my aim. My aim is not what I ought to want or what I think I want, or what is popularly held or unpopularly held to be a worthy object in life, but *what in fact I do want more than anything else.* I have to ask myself, if I embark on what is bound to be difficult work—that is, to become something that I am not, to raise myself to a higher level of existence—am I prepared to pay the price? Is this aim to me more important than fame, riches or the appreciation and admiration of my fellow men, or my own comfort or security, or my bodily desires and needs, or all the other things I may value? Are these more important than my own being? This is simple, common-sense thinking that everyone must undertake for himself, and, moreover, he must try, as far as he can, to be honest about it, realizing always that if we aim at something supremely valuable, we cannot expect it to be cheap.

The second preparatory task is to try, as far as we can, to take stock of our present situation. The first is to decide what I *want;* the second is to decide what I *have* or what I *am.* We can do this to a limited extent even with the few preliminary ideas that we may have, providing we understand one principle, which is the necessity of distinguishing between real and imaginary and of admitting that only what is concrete and verifiable must be accepted as a starting point.

I can see for myself whether I am able to control my own inner states or my external manifestations. I must know whether I can answer the questions most vital to me. I can look at the sufferings of the world—individual and collective—and ask myself whether I have the knowledge or the power to relieve it. I can survey my own future and see before me old age, infirmity and death—and try to penetrate the mystery of life and its meaning and in doing so realize my own ignorance and helplessness. From this, I can turn to the possibility of new knowledge that may perhaps show me the way out and then ask myself once again, "What is such knowledge to me?"

This brings us to the third task, when we are confronted with the hope of finding at least something on which we can rely. Our next duty is clear. It is to verify, as far as we can, whether or not this new factor corresponds to our own needs and our own understanding. No one else can take this responsibility for us, and we have no right to expect that anyone else, whether an individual or an organization, should do so. If I am lost in a forest and somebody claims to show me the way out, I alone must take the responsibility of deciding whether to follow his suggestions or to continue trying on my own, and I shall be wise if I verify as far as possible whether he knows anything about the forest or about orienting himself, whether or not he possesses a compass and a map. If I do not do these things but blindly trust myself to him and subsequently find myself more lost than before, this is my responsibility, and I must reap the consequences of it.

These are elementary, common-sense principles that everyone can and must apply for themselves, as far as this is in their power, before they embark on a way that is new and untried. And what I am going to discuss now must seem a most hazardous undertaking: the application of methods that you have so far not tested and tried, for the attainment of an aim you have not yet truly clarified, and which in any case is almost impossible to describe.

One can, it is true, find various more-or-less satisfying verbal formulations: to change our level of *being;* to attain to life in a world different from the ordinary world of mechanical happenings; to become *real* men and women instead of machines or semianimals, such as we and all people are. But we must realize that, however we may formulate the aim, the implied change in ourselves is so fundamental that we cannot tell its nature in advance. If we have taken these three preliminary questions seriously—we have decided that, such as we are, we know no way out of life and no way out of death, and that to find the way out must be more important to us than turning round and round in this squirrel's cage in which we live—then we have surely come to the point of being prepared at least to experiment with and to see if we can verify methods that claim not merely to show us the way out but enable us to take it.

So we come to the position where we are ready to talk about "how." In the heading of this lecture I put the words "work on oneself" in quotation marks. I write it so because I am used to people saying, "What does this mean?" and professing to be unable to understand how "work on oneself" differs from ordinary attempts to live an upright life. Such people see nothing special in the idea. Others put forward theories about the impossibility of doing anything about oneself, because this would imply an inner division.

I can remember how long it took me personally to understand what is meant by "work on oneself." I have noticed that Ouspensky refers to a similar difficulty in his first contact with Gurdjieff's teaching. A passage at the beginning of *In Search of the Miraculous* describes his first meeting with one of Gurdjieff's groups in Moscow. He says,

> When I asked what was the system they were studying and what were its distinguishing features, I was answered very indefinitely. Then they spoke of 'work on oneself,' but in what this work consisted they failed to explain.

[At this point during the original exposition of the lecture, Mr. Bennett conducted the following experiment:]

I have been thinking how I can try to convey to you what is meant by "work on oneself." It occurred to me to suggest that you should make a simple experiment with me that might help you to make clear one or two things that I want to explain to you this evening. I want each one of you to hold your arms straight above your head.

[Mr. Bennett then held his own arms straight above his head and everyone in the hall (there were about 350 people present) did the same. After a few seconds he said,]

Now stretch your arms as far as you can.

[All the arms then went up by anything up to four inches. Mr.

*Bennett then asked those present to count "one, two, three, four;
four, three, two, one; two, three, four, five; five, four, three, two;
three, four, five, six; six, five, four, three"; and so on. When they
had reached 12 he asked them to stretch their arms again. It was
at once obvious that nearly everyone had allowed their arms to
drop. Mr. Bennett then continued:]*

What do you notice? That when your attention had been taken
away from your arms by putting it to the counting, you relaxed
the effort to straighten them, and when I said, "Straighten your
arms again," all the arms, without exception, went up an inch or
two.

I want to use this to illustrate what I mean by "work on oneself." In the first place, to put your arms above your head was
perhaps to some people an effort, because they thought this was
a ridiculous thing to do in a lecture hall. But nearly everyone
made this effort, whether they thought it ridiculous or not. Then
came an illustration of the relation of our will to our own body.
You put your arms above your heads but—with very few exceptions and those mostly people who had done it before—you did
not make a special effort to straighten them. It was only when I
drew attention to it and said, "Stretch your arms," that you realized there was an additional effort to be made.

So long as you were making this additional effort, most people's arms continued to be straight, but only until we began to
count. Then the effort was diverted from the stretching of your
arms to the counting, and the unusual way of counting engaged
your attention so that you no longer made the effort of stretching
your arms. At the end when I said, "Stretch your arms," almost all
arms straightened and went up an inch or two. Two factors are
involved in this: One is the ability and decision to make a certain
effort, and the second is the work of attention. Even if I decide to
make a certain effort, I can continue only so long as a sufficient
quantity of attention is available.

You will notice that I speak about attention as though it were
something material, and so it is. Attention is matter; it is a particular kind of energy or material of which at any given moment we

have a certain quantity in our organism. When that certain quantity is used up (if we use it faster than we produce it), we cannot, whatever decision we may make, whatever necessity there may be, continue to control our attention. This is generally true of everything we do—all inner and outer processes in the life of man depend upon matter or energy. If we have the necessary material or energy for a process, that process is possible.

Energy is of different kinds. All matter is out of the same kind as wood or coal, which when burned releases its energy merely in the form of heat. Some energy is of a higher kind, more versatile, such as electrical energy. Other energy is connected with excited states of matter. Then there are still higher forms of energy that go beyond the possibility of detection with our ordinary physical apparatus. Everyone who reads even popular books on physics knows that as the frequency of vibrations of radiant energy increases—when the number per second reaches something like one with 20 zeros after it—it scarcely can be perceived at all; it passes through matter, through all the earth's atmosphere, and can hardly be detected. If it had 22 zeros, it would probably pass through quite undetected, and we should have no means of knowing that such energy exists.

There are very good reasons for presuming that there are still higher forms of energy that are not detectable by those types of electrical apparatus that we use today and that, after all, we have used only in relatively recent years. Such energy is connected with experience, with thoughts, with feelings, with sensations and so on. Just as the energy of ordinary thought processes and sensations is a step above the radiant energy that we can detect with our apparatus, the energy with which we have the power of controlling our attention is one step higher than the energy of thoughts, feelings and sensations. And higher than this is still another form of energy that plays a vital part in the life of man. This is the energy that enables us to make decisions, to choose. It is not by the power of thought nor by the power of sensation that we can choose. It is not even with the energy of attention. It is one step higher removed up the scale.

Now, you will ask, "How is this discussion of the different kinds of energy relevant to the problem of self-creation, of *working on ourselves?*" Work on ourselves has, at least as one of its primary purposes, the production in our organism of these higher forms of energy, which in the first place enable us to choose and take real decisions. These higher forms of energy are also able to transform our own functions—thinking, feeling and the rest—and raise them to a higher level. Finally, they can form something in us by which we can live entirely in a different world from the ordinary mechanical world of everyday life.

Before I continue to discuss the work of energy, I shall discuss the psychology of man in as simple terms as possible. We have three primary groups of functions: thinking, feeling and sensing. They work with different parts of our nervous system, using nervous energy that is connected with electrical discharges, and they have the limitations corresponding to this kind of energy. They are no more than very complicated electrical machines, not so very different from those that mathematicians and physicists are constructing in their laboratories.

One of these machines thinks, another feels, while the third is engaged in the activity of the body. The first is connected with the work of the cerebral hemispheres. It is what we usually call our "brain." The second is connected with the sympathetic nervous system, the main center of which is in the solar plexus, and with the other ganglia associated with it. The third is based upon the spinal cord and certain regions in the head. If this were all that existed or could exist in man, he would be no more than a collection of machines—very complicated and able to do very wonderful work, but still no more than machines. But we know that we have some kind of experience or awareness and we know that there is such a thing as attention. What are they? Where do they come from?

The energy with which these three machines usually work is too low in the scale to which I referred to carry with it what we call "experience," that is inner awareness of a process as part of the process itself. For example, you can easily see that your nervous system is constantly receiving impressions from outside, but you are seldom aware of them. If your clothes are comfortable, you do not notice their touch on your body. There are many sounds all the time that you do not hear. There are many thoughts in your mind that you do not notice, feelings that affect your awareness only indirectly. All this constant activity of your three brains can go on—and for the most part does go on—without any experiencing on your part, that is, without any part of you being *aware* of it.

At the same time, experience is possible—it is indeed the only part of our life that is of any immediate importance to us. Experience depends on a higher grade of energy than simple nervous activity. Controlled attention requires a higher grade still. Most of us will sit on a chair and not be aware of the pressure of our bodies on the seat, but if we bring our attention to it, we realize how very little we are aware of what goes on even in our thinking brains, and nearly all that goes on in our feeling brain is what we call unconscious—not associated with attention.

At the same time, these three brains are the whole of our mechanism of response to our environment. It is with them that we live. What we call our conscious experience is mainly associated with our thinking brain, and what is commonly called the unconscious or subconscious is mainly associated with the feeling or sensing parts. This division is quite artificial. We can be quite conscious with these other parts, and we do not realize how little we are conscious of our thinking part. There are certain simple experiments that can be made that will demonstrate to anyone that they are not aware of the thoughts that go on in their thinking brain.

This is the first picture of man. He has three brains, three nervous machines with which he can experience because there is in him the energy of attention. So long as his energy of attention is not controlled from within, his experience is quite automatic and passive. What attracts his attention, he experiences—he is not his own master, but the slave of whatever happens to catch and hold his attention. His experience depends on the accidental activity of his nervous system.

When he begins to control and direct his attention, then to some extent he experiences what he wants to experience. For example, if I direct my attention towards my thoughts, I can think what I decide to think and not what happens to come into my mind, but if I do not make this effort of attention, my thoughts can be only automatic associations—verbal associations, and so on—and what I will be thinking a minute hence is quite unpredictable. That is the ordinary state of the working of the thinking brain. It is by attention that intentional experience comes, that control, and therefore change, becomes possible.

But attention alone does not give freedom. Attention alone is not the same thing as "will." What we ordinarily call "will" is merely the result of all the forces that work on our attention and pull us this way and that way. "Real will" is connected with the higher energy about which I spoke, in which there is the power of *effective decision*. This implies, at the very least, full power over our own organism. It implies much else besides, but for the moment I am concerned with the primary necessity that my "I" should have power over my thoughts, feelings and sensations, and my bodily reactions in general. For ordinary people, the impulse for their thoughts, feelings and bodies comes from their desires, their attractions and aversions. These are, of course, held within the limits imposed by training and habit; but, so far as the setting in motion or activation of all these bodily and psychic processes is concerned, the active principles are the forces of desire and aversion, attraction and repulsion. In so far as *these* control us, *we* control nothing, for they arise without our will or intention.

Now let me try to sort out this rough sketch I have been giving you. The first picture is of man as a being who has three mechanisms for living, three mechanisms for response to the external world: thinking, feeling, sensing.

The work of the three brains can be quite automatic, without any intention or purpose, or it can be controlled either through the direction of attention or in a still higher way through the presence of something that is independent of both the brains and the attention. I have thus made, in two ways, a threefold division of man. The first is a division of man into three parts as far as mechanical functions are concerned, and the second is into three parts as far as his possible level of experience is concerned. Such a classification is sufficient to explain the methods of work, but I must say at once that it is very much simplified and when you come to study it in detail, many adjustments and corrections will have to be made. I am at this stage using only a first approximation to enable me to introduce these ideas to you.

The next question that we have to ask now is where, in this, am *I?* What is *myself* in all this? Is myself either the whole or part of my thinking brain? Is myself my feelings, my emotional states, my likes and dislikes? Or is myself my body and all the experience of my body, that is, what I call the sensing brain or sensing mechanism? If you will take the trouble to study and verify what I have been saying, you will see that these three brains nearly always work out of contact with one another and are unaware of one another, so that if this self is in one brain, then it is not in another. This is one of the easiest things to verify. It thus quickly becomes clear that we cannot say, "I am my thoughts," "I am my feelings" or "I am my body," and yet I talk about myself as "I." This either implies that there is something in me that is separate from and over and above my thoughts, feelings and sensations, or else that I am talking about something that does not exist.

My "I" is my will. It is my existence as a free being. It is that which redeems me from the emptiness of a mere machine. But I have no "I"—my experience is a mere succession of accidental states induced by external shocks. Gurdjieff compares man to a taxi, whom any fare can pick up and drive wherever he pleases. A man with a real "I" is like a car with an owner, who is always one and the same. We have to saturate ourselves with the realization of this distinction.

I am not a machine because my brains are mechanical but because I have no "I" to control and direct my brains. Of course, we know that a philosopher once said, "I think, therefore I am." But the truth is that "I" do not think—"it thinks" in me. My experience of the thinking (or feeling or sensing for that matter) that goes on in me is something accidental and uncontrolled.

Because of this, there is nothing in me that can take decisions in any real sense of the term. Thoughts about decisions or feelings about decisions may arise in me, but by the time that action has to be taken, I may have no awareness at all of the present or no memory of the past. Only he who can say, "I am" today, yesterday and tomorrow—the same one and indivisible—can be said to have an "I." When we begin to make an honest survey of the situation, we are forced to admit that no such "I" exists in us. We cannot even picture to ourselves what such an "I" could be.

If there is not the "I" in me that should exist in a man worthy of the name, why is it absent? How should it have arisen? Gurdjieff answers ". . .in childhood, during the period of preparation for responsible age." We are taxis because our machine was never put into the hands of its real owner. The very thing that is the most necessary and essential part of a person, *that he should be capable of taking responsible decisions,* is absent even from people who most appear to have it and pride themselves on having it. They confuse the automatic working of their three brains, which comes from training and habit, with real will, with the real power of independent decision.

Why do both philosophers and ordinary people talk about man and about themselves as if they had an "I"? Why do they believe in something that, according to what I have been saying, does not exist? The answer is that they want to believe it, and therefore they call whatever experience happens to be present by the name of "I," even if it is quite unconnected with what was there a minute before and even if it will change into something quite different a minute later. All this is called by Gurdjieff the "imaginary I" in man, and he calls a man who has no real "I" a "man in quotation marks" and not a real man at all.

No doubt you will have found it hard to accept and perhaps even to understand what I have been saying. That does not matter for the moment. I wanted only to introduce two or three ideas that are necessary for the subject matter of this lecture. I had to say something about the three brain, and about the distinction between the real and the illusory self because practical methods are concerned with harmonizing and balancing these three brains so that they can work together, not separately, and with the discarding of the illusory or false self and the finding or formation of an "I," a real self.

The picture of a real man is that of a being who has an "I" that is an unchanging center of decision in himself, who can take decisions that are valid not only for this moment but for tomorrow, next year and for the rest of his life, if necessary, and who, moreover, is able to take decisions not only for one brain but for all three—whereas people like ourselves can do no more than take decisions that affect one of our brains at a time. Now how is a man to have such an "I" if it cannot exist in one of the brains without putting that brain out of balance with the rest? Evidently he must have something in him that exists, that holds together, apart from his own nervous system—apart even from his own bodily organism.

This brings us to an idea that is very ancient, but that has taken so many distorted forms that we must try to formulate it clearly. This is the idea of the "higher bodies" of man. Every kind of theory about higher bodies in man has been put forward: that man has astral, mental, causal or many other bodies; or that he can have a second body, the "Resurrection Body" of the Pauline Epistles. Sometimes, instead of the word "body" such words as "soul" or "spirit" are used. But in every case they imply something that is not of the same stuff as the physical body.

Whatever name may be given to this "something" that is the seat of the real man—of his "I"—people agree either that he has it and that all men have it, or that it is a mere fiction and does not exist in anyone. Gurdjieff does not teach either the one or the other. He says we *can* have higher bodies or souls, but in order to have them they must be created by our own work. He teaches that man is born and lives, so far as the ordinary mechanical level of existence is concerned, with only one body—the ordinary physical body, obeying physical and mechanical laws. That body, like every other material object, is subject to decay in time and at death disintegrates and disappears and has no further unified existence.

At the same time, man can form in himself a second body, which is made of a higher order of matter than his physical body. It is, in fact, just through this body, when it exists, that *unified* instead of dispersed experience is possible. The attention of a man without the second body can never separate itself from his three brains and stand apart from them. It is the second body that can have true voluntary attention, real power over thoughts, feelings and bodily experience.

This second body is formed in man as a result of a certain kind of struggle that I am going to discuss. In those who have it, its existence can be verified not only by psychological but even by physical tests. When the physical body dies, then, the second body does not disintegrate because it is not made of the same material.

At the same time, it is not the vehicle of the true self, the independent will. These belong to the third body in man. This is made from the highest form of energy, which—to avoid going into the very long descriptions connecting it in your minds with misleading associations—I call the energy of will, or energy of "decision." When the third body is formed, a man becomes in the full sense of the word a free being. He has complete power over himself. He can exist without dependence on the first or physical body. The third body is the seat of the will, and without the third body there can be only evanescent, transitory will—there cannot be any permanent will in man. The third body is the soul in the Christian sense. It is the "wedding garment" of the parable. It is of the third body that Christ speaks when He says, "What shall it profit a man if he gain the whole world and lose his own soul?"

You may remember that in the first lecture I spoke about two different destinies for man: Either he can have the destiny of animals, on the deterministic level, or he can raise himself to a second level in which not only his own existence is different, but in which his relations with other people are also different. This is a simplification, because there is more than one level possible, but roughly speaking we can say that the man who has the second body actually exists in a different world from the man who has only a first body, and the man with a third body exists in a different world and has a different present and a different future from the man who exists only in two or in the one body. Fully balanced, "normal" existence for man is the existence in which he has three bodies and independent experience in each of the three bodies. This is attainable not by a change of experience alone, but by a chemical process.

Let me explain why I call it a "chemical process." The chemist takes certain materials, lets them act on one another under approximate conditions and obtains other compounds that are more valuable, the whole process being subject to natural quantitative laws. There is always a certain price to be paid for what he does: He either has to put energy into the process, or he has to discard something in the course of getting what he wants.

It is exactly this that is involved in the process of creation of our own being. A man is like a chemical factory. He takes in three different kinds of raw material: the food we eat, the air we breathe, and the impressions that come into us through our sense organs. These are all sources of energy. We are familiar with the idea that our food is transformed into energy in our bodies. The air we breathe not only takes part in the simple process of producing heat energy, but in more complicated chemical processes it builds up substances necessary for our life and for these higher energies about which I have spoken. Every time that a nerve ending is stimulated by light, heat, touch or whatever it may be, a corresponding energy enters my body and there is a nervous discharge.

Ordinary people make no use at all of the possibilities of their chemical factory and even destroy its products. They are like a very unproductive, wasteful factory that employs thousands of operatives and manages to do no more than keep the factory itself supplied with raw material, with nothing to sell and nothing to store. They use up all the energy they produce without gaining anything at all, either for themselves or for any higher purpose or for the good of their neighbors.

If we wish to increase the output of this human chemical factory, we must work on two things. There are two main departments where the working of the factory can be changed. The first is the department of *attention*. The alchemists, who used their own terminology to describe various psychological things (the word alchemy means "psychological transformation" in man), used the word "quicksilver," and they used to say one has to "learn to fix one's quicksilver."

We have to learn how to bring this very wayward energy of attention, so subtle and so hard to hold, under control. If we do this, certain changes take place in the inner working of our organism. When I direct and hold my attention, a transformation of energy takes place that produces material that can be used for various purposes. First of all, energy is used up in my psychic activity and in the life of my body. Secondly, I am constantly radiating energy out into space. This energy is not wasted but is needed for the general purposes of life. If I make the effort to control my attention, the quality of my radiation changes, and this has an important result about which Gurdjieff has much to say in his writings. Then there is the third use of energy of attention, which is for the formation and growth of my higher bodies.

The second department in the chemical factory, whose work must be made more effective, deals with even stronger forces than the power of attention. I am going to speak about only one aspect of this energy: the force of sacrifice or suffering. In suffering, there is a transformation of energy of a higher order. If I am the slave of my own egoism, then the energy liberated by suffering will go into some such process as self-pity, worry, fear, anger, irritation, indignation, jealousy and envy, and it will be quite wasted as far as I am concerned.

Now, this energy happens to be of very special value—it is one of the foods of my own higher body. Whether I wish it or not, I must produce this energy, that is, I must suffer. But it is in my own hands to make this suffering useful. If I do not do so, it is not merely wasted, it actually becomes a poison and can do me great harm, even in my ordinary mechanical existence. We all know how quickly men and women degenerate once they give themselves up to suffering, whether it is self-pity and anxiety or whether it is violent in the form of anger and hatred. We have equally clear evidence of the positive results of suffering that is not allowed to flow into egoistic channels. The best and most beautiful characters we meet in our ordinary life are nearly always moulded by suffering rightly borne.

So far, I have spoken only of "involuntary suffering," that is suffering that comes without our choice or intention. This has only limited possibilities, for it can never be wholly conscious. Quite different results can be gained from what Gurdjieff calls "voluntary suffering."

There are certain changes that it is necessary for me to bring about in myself which can be obtained only if I intentionally, of my own decision, put myself into a situation of suffering. I have many weaknesses, many defective processes, and the combination of these weaknesses and defects with my own imaginary self—my imaginary "I," the picture I have of myself—brings me into a state of almost complete slavery. On the one hand, I cannot overcome my weaknesses, and on the other, I cannot give up my picture of myself as not weak.

Between these two I am constrained to pretend to myself and to pretend to other people, to hide all the time what I really know to be present, and to try to show what does not really exist—in short, to live a life of lies. In this condition, no liberation of the higher energy is possible, because whatever energy is developed will inevitably flow into the channels of jealousy, self-pity, irritation, anger and the rest. If I understand this, I see that there is nothing for it but to put myself into such a situation that this constraining channel of weakness on the one side and self-love on the other will be broken down. In doing so, not only shall I prevent this energy from being lost, but I shall actually bring about a more complete transformation, by which the building up of the material needed for the higher body can be accelerated sufficiently to achieve it within the time that is available to me.

This is the general conception of the process of self-creation in man. Gurdjieff calls it "conscious labour and intentional suffering," and it runs like a golden thread throughout his writings. I have tried only to give you some idea of the meaning of this phrase, of the kind of effort and work it implies.

I shall not say more about these general methods in these lectures for they are important only when they are taken practically—and they can be taken practically only when they have been understood and the necessity for "work on oneself" has penetrated into one's very being. Before I conclude this lecture, I want to give you some account of special methods that occupy an important place in Gurdjieff's teaching. You will have already understood that work on attention and the effort to overcome the resistances of our own organism are necessary elements in "work on oneself." We also have to learn how to develop the powers latent in our three brains and bring them into harmony with one another.

Gurdjieff studied particularly and taught as a very important part of his whole work methods for developing, harmonizing and unifying the three brains through physical work. These methods are called for convenience "movements." They were brought together by Gurdjieff from many Eastern and a few Western schools that have studied the use of rhythmic movements and sacred dances, and they form a very important part of his teaching. As I have already stated, he was long known in Asia as the greatest authority on temple dancing. Perhaps some of you have seen demonstrations of the movements. The movements are one important and valuable feature of his teaching. They shorten considerably the work of studying, in the first instance, then of becoming conscious and of eventually being able to use the three brains rightly and in harmony. To help people to find and understand the working of their feeling and sensing parts, use of a special kind of music is made. Gurdjieff made a very profound study of music and the use of vibrations in general and the part they play in human life.

Then, as regards the psychological study of man—that is, the means by which one can study oneself and other people—he devised a detailed system of psychology that I will not speak about because you can read about it in Ouspensky's *In Search of the Miraculous.*

Gurdjieff had certain other special methods of conveying that deeper knowledge that is too subtle to be put into ordinary verbal formulae. He made very great use of more than one special kind of symbolism. Some of these are described in Ouspensky's *In Search of the Miraculous.* In his own book in the first series of his writings, he makes use of a number of different symbolisms, one within another, so that quite simple ideas are expressed, but the more deeply you study, the more subtle ideas you find within these. For teaching people in contact with him, he often used to employ a symbolism created on the spur of the moment for those who could understand it. Sometimes one might see 30 or 40 people in the room, of whom each understood quite differently what he intended to tell them because he would use a symbolism of a form that would evoke different responses in different people.

In this way, there was a progression in his methods of teaching that corresponds to what he called three circles or three degrees. He calls these three the "exoteric," the "mesoteric" and the "esoteric," or the outer, middle and inner circles. A person who comes in contact with his ideas and who, having answered for himself the three preliminary questions about which I spoke, has decided that he wishes to learn has entered the exoteric or outer circle. For those in this circle, a certain kind of knowledge and a certain kind of method are available. Those who satisfy themselves and also show by their life that this can give objectively the results they are seeking pass into the second circle. This involves quite different demands, and those in it can receive quite different help. One may say that in the first or exoteric circle no demands are made, because no demands can be made of people who understand nothing and have no control over themselves. When people begin to understand and have a certain degree of control over themselves and want more and are prepared to pay more, different kinds of relationships can be established. The third or inner circle is that in which the pupil comes to grips with reality. Once he enters it, he must hold onto it until he achieves his aim.

The work that starts inside—at the root of my own nature—must by degrees find its way out. Firstly, into my dealings with those nearest to me. Next, into my relations with my fellowmen in general. Ultimately, I may hope that it will lead me step by step to discover and realize the sense of my existence and bring me face to face with my Creator.

"THE SOLE MEANS NOW for the saving of the beings of the planet Earth would be to implant again into their presences a new organ . . . of such properties that every one of these unfortunates during the process of existence should constantly sense and be cognizant of the inevitability of his own death, as well as of the death of everyone upon whom his eyes or attention rests."

—From the last chapter of *Beelzebub's Tales to His Grandson*.

Chapter 4

Gurdjieff's Writings

IN THE ACCOUNT OF GURDJIEFF'S LIFE AND WORK that I gave in the second lecture, I said that he had composed three series of writings designed to lead the reader step by step to an understanding of what is meant by "work on oneself." At the end of the last lecture, I referred to his division of his pupils into three groups or circles according to their degree of practical understanding of this work. It will, no doubt, have occurred to you that there must be some connection between these two sequences of three; the word "esoteric" may have conveyed to you the idea of something in his writings hidden from the profane and revealed only to "initiates."

Before we begin to speak about Gurdjieff's writings, I want to say a little about his attitude to what is commonly called "esotericism." We are used to hearing such words as "esoteric" or "occult." and they very easily lead to misunderstanding. They can be taken in quite a wrong way, as if to imply that some kind of important knowledge is deliberately hidden from people or that access to it is intentionally made more difficult than it need be; or as if there were different kinds of knowledge, one kind of knowledge reserved for special people and other kinds of knowledge that are inferior and open to everyone. These are quite wrong distinctions. Real knowledge, even the highest possible knowledge, is no more hidden from people than, let us say, the most advanced mathematics is hidden from people in a university. Anyone who wishes may go and hear the most abstruse lectures of which they cannot understand a single word, and this obviously brings no profit to them unless they are prepared to work through the preparatory stages. Until they are able to understand and use delicate subtle mathematical operations, it is quite useless for them to attend lectures by the great and famous teachers.

There is no essential difference in the communication of knowledge connected with the destiny of man and the ultimate reality, except that it is not always so obvious that we do not understand what is being taught. If I were going to lecture on the calculus of tensors and you came in by mistake to see me writing a lot of symbols and formulae on the blackboard, those of you who were not specialists in the subject would realize that you had come to the wrong place and ask for your money back. But suppose someone were speaking about the really deep secrets of human nature; you would miss even more completely the real sense of what they were saying, but you would probably imagine you understood and so would give a quite wrong meaning to it. That would happen because the language in which they would speak about such things would necessarily be very subtle and elusive in order to convey the fine distinctions that are characteristic of ultimate reality.

Such fine distinctions cannot be expressed in the rough-and-ready formulae of our ordinary conversation. Conversations may take place in which very important and yet very subtle matters are discussed, and people may take a great deal of trouble and push themselves forward in order to be present at such conversations, thinking to gain something by it. It then usually happens that they not only miss the whole point of what is being said, but often understand something quite different, sometimes even dan-gerous to themselves.

Real knowledge has to be approached by stages, and especially real knowledge of an ultimate character. Gurdjieff described these stages in three very broad divisions, and I am going to speak about this first, before we come to his writings. Real knowledge can be conveyed from one person to another on three different levels. To these Gurdjieff gave the names "philosophical," "theoretical" and "practical."

The first and lowest of these is the philosophical level. Truth on this level can be conveyed only in terms of general principles, as a way of understanding. It does not approach the complexity and subtlety of actual facts and actual experience.

On the second or theoretical level, fundamental laws can be taught and learned. Once these laws are understood, it is possible to use them to solve particular problems. This is a great step forward from the first or philosophical stage. I do not mean that knowledge on the philosophical level has no value in practical life, but it has value only as a general guide, and many of the concrete problems that arise in actual life are not at all soluble in philosophical terms—too many factors are involved. The problem is too small in relation to the greatness of the whole.

It is only on the practical level that everything becomes concrete. Here every individual can see himself as he really is and his position in relation to others, and to the universe as a whole. Problems can be solved in such a way that there is no distinction between *knowing* and *doing*. There is not the distinction that we commonly draw between knowing what we should do and knowing how to do it.

The universe is very large and subject to laws of different grades. These laws interpenetrate and pass from one level to another. They become very complicated indeed by the time anything so small as individual man is reached. The complexity of the laws operating in the life of one individual man or woman is so great that often no solution of the practical problems of life can be found in philosophical or theoretical terms. It is only on a very advanced level that the problems of the individual can be seen in a way of thinking. We imagine that the problems of individuals are within the compass of our understanding. We may even think it more difficult to understand great laws than to understand one man. It is not so.

Gurdjieff constructed the written exposition of his teaching in a form that corresponds to this division of levels of understanding. He wrote three series of books, one that deals with general principles, one that deals with theory, and the third that deals with the actual practice of the transformation of man. The first series is not a treatise on philosophy in the sense in which we should ordinarily understand it. It is concerned, as philosophy should be, with the reconstruction of our thought, with furnishing people with "valid categories," as they are called, which are sound materials for thinking; and it is concerned, above all, with getting rid of all faulty material that obstructs our thinking. Our modern world is far from any real understanding of the sense and significance of human life and still further, by a very long way, from any possibility of doing anything effective to bring human life into normal channels. The objective of the first series is therefore necessarily more critical than constructive, more to get rid of false conceptions about man than to furnish material for a new world.

At the very beginning of the first series of his writings, Gurdjieff sets out the objectives of each of the three series, which exist under the collective title *All and Everything*. I am going to quote the text of the title page for you as an introduction to what I am going to say further:*

All and Everything

FIRST SERIES: Three books under the title of *"An Objectively Impartial Criticism of the Life of Man,"* or, *"Beelzebub's Tales to His Grandson."*

SECOND SERIES: Three books under the common title of *"Meetings With Remarkable Men."*

THIRD SERIES: Four books under the common title of *"Life is Real Only Then, When 'I Am'."*

All written according to entirely new principles of logical

---

* [The grammar and punctuation in this and subsequent quotations from Gurdjieff's writings remain as they were published in the original editions.]

reasoning and strictly directed towards the solution of the following three cardinal problems:

FIRST SERIES: To destroy, mercilessly, without any compromises whatsoever, in the mentation and feelings of the reader, the beliefs and views, by centuries rooted in him, about everything existing in the world.

SECOND SERIES: To acquaint the reader with the material required for a new creation and to prove the soundness and good quality of it.

THIRD SERIES: To assist the arising, in the mentation and in the feelings of the reader, of a veritable, nonfantastic representation not of that illusory world which he now perceives, but of the world existing in reality.

I shall start with the first series: *An Objectively Impartial Criticism of the Life of Man* or, as it will be convenient to call it, *Beelzebub.* This is an extraordinary book in every sense of the word. Gurdjieff devoted immense effort and time to its writing and revision. It is a long book—more than a thousand pages of print, and every page is important. To those who have read and studied it deeply—and it is worth mentioning that many of Gurdjieff's pupils have read it from cover to cover 20 times or more—it is an inexhaustible source of new knowledge and inspiration.

The purpose of the book is to help the reader to divest himself of his humanistic, geocentric attitude towards the problems of the universe and arrive at an objective standpoint. This is commonly supposed to be the task of the philosophers, and you might expect to find a closely reasoned book in which history, psychology and sociology are analysed on the basis of some philosophical principle. Many such books have been written, and they have changed little or nothing in the life of man. Gurdjieff's book deals with historical, psychological and sociological questions, but not by way of analysis and discussion. He has chosen for his exposition the form of a narrative relating the experiences of a being from another planet who visits the earth and studies the life of mankind. It can be conceived as a vast allegory into which historical and scientific information of immense interest is introduced, as well as theoretical and practical teaching about human psychology and "work on oneself." I shall try to give you some idea of the form and content of the book, but before doing so I must not fail to emphasize the difficulty of reading it.

In the first place, the language is unfamiliar. New words are introduced to convey ideas that are quite new to our modern thought or to give a fresh turn to old ideas. At first, the unfamiliarity of these new words produces a disconcerting impression, but this soon wears off and for most readers ceases to be much of an obstacle. Far more difficult is the form of the narrative itself. Sometimes the stories are very simple and touching; at other times they convey an exceedingly subtle and elusive teaching. The narrative is not continuous, the thread often being broken to insert and emphasize some special idea. Much is conveyed in the form of dramatic pictures or allegories. It is almost impossible to tell without very deep and persistent study what is meant to be taken literally, what allegorically and what in the form of a special symbolism. Many of the formulations are so compressed that no one could understand them without reference to other passages. The most important and valuable teaching is often introduced by way of a passage that at first glance seems a mere repetition of something that has been said before.

These are not the only difficulties in reading *Beelzebub*. The central ideas are themselves very hard to understand and accept. Even when all that is said on a given subject is pieced together and studied, there remains a quality that eludes any ordinary intellectual approach. Often I have seen highly educated people with a wide reading in the subject discussed, completely nonplussed by a passage that a simple person approaching the subject only from feeling and common sense immediately understands and accepts. *Beelzebub* is difficult, but not in the sense that the *Summa Theologia* or the *Critique of Pure Reason* are difficult. It requires no special education or training—but it does make a peculiar demand on the reader: that he should sincerely desire to know and that he should be prepared to feel and sense as well as to think. Whoever is prepared to persevere will gain from his reading of *Beelzebub* that change of attitude towards himself and his destiny that is the necessary condition for "work on oneself."

But the difficulties of *Beelzebub* are not only intellectual. There are obstacles of quite a different kind in the subject matter itself. From start to finish the book outrages any susceptibilities the reader may have. The scientist is contemptuous of the dogmatic assertions that appear inconsistent with the most firmly established scientific "facts." The historian is amused or irritated at the disregard for all accepted chronology and the claim, made throughout the book, that the true course of history has been on quite different lines from what is generally accepted. The philologist can make no sense of the linguistic usage, nor the anthropologist of the statements about races and the migrations of peoples. The artist is pilloried as a useless degenerate, and all our modern art denounced as an altogether harmful factor in human life. Religious susceptibilities are wounded by accounts of the life and work of the founders of the great religions that are quite contrary to current beliefs. Our Western notions of good taste are shocked by the open discussion of problems of sex and human relationships generally. National susceptibilities are outraged by merciless satires upon the life and customs of the various countries of the world. Our ideas of literary style are set at nought. Finally, there runs through the book a note of arrogant superiority that is utterly offensive to our notions of "good form." It is safe to say that no reader, at a first perusal of the book, will reach the last page without having been shocked and outraged at some point.

All this is obviously deliberate and an essential part of the whole plan. It is fundamental for the very approach that Gurdjieff makes to the human problem of the present day, that mankind is completely astray and that there is nothing—literally nothing—in our science, art, philosophy, religion or political and social systems that is not tainted through and through with false notions about man, with egoism and self-deception. I can assure you from my own experience of hundreds of people who have read *Beelzebub* with persistent attention that it helps them towards an objective and impartial attitude towards man better than any amount of explanation or advice.

Before reading you some typical passages, I will try and give you a summary of the narrative portions of the book as a whole.

The hero of the story is Beelzebub, who is represented as an angel or devil who, in his youth, revolted against what he conceived to be an injustice in the universe. In consequence of this he was exiled from the Center of the Universe to a very remote place, our solar system. He lived on the planet Mars, but from time to time, visited the Earth. His first descent was at the time of Atlantis, 12,000 years ago. From time to time, through the great civilizations of Egypt, Tikliamish, Babylon and so on to recent times, further visits are made.

Nearly the whole of the book consists of a narrative of Beelzebub's six descents upon the planet Earth. The tales are told to his grandson, Hassein, whose upbringing he has taken under his care. Man and his history are used by Beelzebub as illustrative material to develop in Hassein the power of impartial reasoning and compassion for suffering.

Man is described as a "three-brained being," with a special kind of destiny, differing from the destiny of two- or one-brained beings (animals and invertebrates) in that the possession of three brains gives the power of choice. With this comes the possibility of self-creation, of forming in oneself true, imperishable individuality. It is taken for granted that such beings exist on many planets in the universe and that most, if not all of them, have reached a higher level of development than man.

Our earth is presented as a particularly unfortunate planet, where, owing to accidental, unforeseen events connected with the formation of our moon, the development of organic life on the earth passed through a long, unfavorable period. This lasted many thousands of years corresponding to most of what geologists call the "Quaternary Period," when man had already appeared, but when it was not yet possible for man to exercise his true function—that is, a being capable of developing himself.

Because of this unpropitious situation existing on the earth, it was necessary to protect man from the realization of what he was missing, to protect him from the knowledge that he was different from the animal, and yet was unable to enter into possession of that very thing that made him different. This "spiritual sterilization," as it were, of the higher possibilities of man, is described by Beelzebub as the implanting in our remote ancestors of a special organ connected with part of the nervous system that prevented man from seeing things as they really are, which made him see his destiny in terms only of his animal existence, and although he had the third brain—the power of thought—to use that only for the purposes of the animal existence. This organ is called the "organ Kundabuffer," a word of fantastic etymology taken partly from a Sanskrit word meaning "coiled" and also "a snake." Kundabuffer is stated to have been removed from man by a process of breeding at a time when the relations between the moon and the earth had been so stabilized that this "spiritual sterilization" was no longer necessary.

However, owing to the long period of time, tens of thousands of years, during which this organ had been present in these remote ancestors of ours, certain consequences had become inherent and remained as a predisposition towards self-deception and the inability to see things as they really are. Although man was liberated, he failed to use his liberty in the right way. This may be conceived as a way of expressing the theological notion of the "Fall of Man." In consequence, man lost the power to raise himself to the level of existence that he should occupy by his own essential nature, that is, the essential nature of a self-creating being. This is the general conception of man that Beelzebub put before Hassein.

This unfortunate, tragic situation of mankind on the earth is further represented as having attracted the attention of the higher levels in the universe and even of our All-Merciful Creator. The Creator Himself has, from time to time, sent messengers, beings of a higher nature than man, sons of God, who incarnate on the earth in human form. In this form, they endeavor to reopen for man the way to liberation from the consequences of his early failure.

Many of the early chapters are devoted to accounts of different ways in which this task has been undertaken. Beelzebub himself is represented not as being directly concerned in these great tasks, but as having been entrusted from time to time with special undertakings on the earth, as, for example, to combat the spread of animal sacrifice, which was both disastrous for man and contrary to the whole meaning of man's relation with the higher powers. A number of chapters are concerned with the various measures Beelzebub took—the lines he followed in India, Central Asia and elsewhere to try to put an end to animal sacrifices. This is represented as having happened thousands of years ago, when animal sacrifices had reached disastrous proportions. Not only the killing of animals but the killing of man is taken as a disastrous feature of human life and, indeed, as the greatest of evils on the earth. War is a most unnatural process, contrary to the nature of three-brained beings. Beelzebub is shown in the third book studying and trying to understand how it is possible that man can fall into such states that war is possible. One of the final chapters deals with war and the causes and prevention of war, about which I said a little in the first of these lectures.

This is the general thread running through the book: of man as a being unfortunate in relation to the general conditions of life on the earth but compensated to a great extent for this misfortune by the intervention of beings sent from Above. In connection with the practical issues, there are a number of stories illustrating the impossibility of achieving right results by wrong methods, by violence and by mere external organizations in which the people concerned in the organization remain themselves unchanged. There is also one very beautiful and striking series of chapters describing the legendary being Ashiata Shiemash, who is described as born of the Sumerian race before the rise of Babylon. He is represented as having, for a short period, inaugurated and maintained on the earth normal conditions among people, not by external organization but by having brought home to people the necessity for self-efforts, for work on the creation of their own being.

I propose to quote for you one or two passages that would be illustrative of this first series, and I have chosen a short passage from this very chapter. Ashiata Shiemash, who is represented as one of the beings incarnated from Above perhaps 5,000 years ago, is described by Beelzebub as having studied the human problem closely in order to decide by what means he could re-new the realization of the necessity for man to struggle for his own self-perfection. He has examined the three Sacred Impulses in man from which this striving should come—Faith, Hope and Love. At the point where I shall begin to quote, he has been stud-ying these and meditating on the results of his studies, and then he says, quoting a record that was supposed to have been made by Ashiata Shiemash himself and later found by Beelzebub and studied by him:

> "These meditations of mine made it categorically clear to me, that all the genuine function proper to men-beings, as they are proper to all the three-centered beings of our Great Universe, had already degenerated in their remote ancestors into other functions, namely, into func-tions included among the properties of the organ Kunda-buffer which were very similar to the genuine sacred be-ing-functions of Faith, Love, and Hope.

> "And this degeneration occurred in all probability in consequence of the fact that when the organ Kundabuf-fer had been destroyed in these ancestors, and they had also acquired in themselves factors for the genuine sa-cred being-impulses, then, as the taste of many of the properties of the organ Kundabuffer still remained in them, these properties of the organ Kundabuffer which resembled these three sacred impulses became gradually mixed with the latter, with the result that there were crys-tallized in their psyche the factors for the impulses Faith, Love and Hope, which although similar to the genuine, were nevertheless somehow or other quite distinct.

> "The contemporary three-centered beings here do at times believe, love, and hope with their Reason as well as

with their feelings; but how they believe, how they love, and how they hope—ah, it is exactly in this that all the peculiarity of these three being-properties lies!

"They also believe, but this sacred impulse in them does not function independently, as it does in general in all the three-centered beings existing on the various other planets of our Great Universe, upon which beings with the same possibilities breed; but it arises dependent upon some or other factors, which have been formed in their common presences, owing as always to the same consequences of the properties of the organ Kundabuffer—as for instance, the particular properties arising in them which they call 'vanity,' 'self-love,' 'pride,' 'self-conceit,' and so forth.

"In consequence of this, the three-brained beings here are for the most part subject just to the perceptions and fixations in their presences of all sorts of 'Sinkrpoosarams' or, as it is expressed here, they 'believe-any-old-tale.'

"It is perfectly easy to convince beings of this planet of anything you like, provided only during their perceptions of these 'fictions,' there is evoked in them and there proceeds, either consciously from without, or automatically by itself, the functioning of one or another corresponding consequence of the properties of the organ Kundabuffer crystallized in them from among those that form what is called the 'subjectivity' of the given being, as for instance: 'self-love,' 'vanity,' 'pride,' 'swagger,' 'imagination,' 'bragging,' 'arrogance,' and so on.

"From the influence of such actions upon their degenerated Reason and on the degenerated factors in their localizations, which factors actualize their being-sensations, not only is there crystallized a false conviction concerning the mentioned fictions, but thereafter in all sincerity and faith, they will even vehemently prove to those around them, that it is just so and can in no way be otherwise.

"In an equally abnormal form were data moulded in them for evoking the sacred impulse of love.

"In the presences of the beings of contemporary times, there also arises and is present in them as much as you please of that strange impulse which they call love; but this love of theirs is firstly also the result of certain crystallized consequences of the properties of the same Kundabuffer; and secondly this impulse of theirs arises and manifests itself in the process of every one of them entirely subjectively; so subjectively and so differently that if ten of them were asked to explain how they sensed this inner impulse of theirs, then all ten of them—if, of course, they for once replied sincerely, and frankly confessed their genuine sensations and not those they had read about somewhere or had obtained from somebody else—all ten would reply differently and describe ten different sensations.

"One would explain this sensation in the sexual sense; another the sense of pity; a third in the sense of desire for submission; a fourth, in a common craze for outer things, and so on and so forth; but not one of the ten could describe even remotely, the sensation of genuine Love.

"And none of them would, because in none of the ordinary beings-men here has there ever been for a long time, any sensation of the sacred being-impulse of genuine Love. And without this 'taste' they cannot even vaguely describe that most beatific sacred being-impulse in the presence of every three-centered being of the whole Universe, which, in accordance with the divine foresight of Great Nature, forms those data in us, from the result of the experiencing of which we can blissfully rest from the meritorious labors actualized by us for the purpose of self-perfection.

"Here, in these times, if one of those three-brained beings 'loves' somebody or other, then he loves him either because the latter always encourages and undeservingly flatters him; or because his nose is much like the nose of that female or male, with whom thanks to the cosmic law of 'polarity' or 'type' a relation has been established which has not yet been broken; or finally, he loves him only because the latter's uncle is in a big way of business and may one day give him a boost, and so on and so forth.

"But never do beings-men here love with genuine, impartial, and nonegoistic love.

"Thanks to this kind of love in the contemporary beings here, their hereditary predispositions to the crystallizations of the consequences of the properties of the organ Kundabuffer are crystallized at the present time without hindrance, and finally become fixed in their nature as a lawful part of them.

"And as regards the third sacred being-impulse, namely, 'essence-hope,' its plight in the presences of the three-centered beings here is even worse than with the first two.

"Such a being-impulse has not only finally adapted itself in them to the whole of their presences in a distorted form, but this maleficent strange 'hope' newly formed in them, which has taken the place of the being-impulse of Sacred Hope, is now already the principal reason why factors can no longer be acquired in them for the functioning of the genuine being-impulses of Faith, Love, and Hope.

"In consequence of this newly-formed-abnormal hope of theirs, they always hope in something; and thereby all those possibilities are constantly being paralyzed in them, which arise in them either intentionally from without or accidentally by themselves, which possibilities could perhaps still destroy in their presences their hereditary predispositions to the crystallizations of the consequences of the properties of the organ Kundabuffer.

"When I returned from the mountain Veziniama to the city of Babylon, I continued my observations in order to make it clear whether it was not possible somehow or other to help these unfortunates in some other way.

"During the period of my year of special observations on all of their manifestations and perceptions, I made it categorically clear to myself that although the factors for engendering in their presences the sacred being-impulses of Faith, Hope, and Love are already quite degenerated in the beings of this planet, nevertheless, the factor which ought to engender that being-impulse on which the whole psyche of beings of a three-brained system is in general based, and which impulse exists under the name of Objective-Conscience, is not yet atrophied in them, but remains in their presences almost in its primordial state.

"Thanks to the abnormally established conditions of external ordinary being-existence existing here, this factor has gradually penetrated and become embedded in that consciousness which is here called 'subconsciousness,' in consequence of which it takes no part whatever in the functioning of their ordinary consciousness.'

That is a fairly typical passage. As you see, the language is at first difficult, but it is an idiom to which one becomes accustomed when reading it. At the same time, I must warn you that this passage is comparatively simple, compared with others, in the number of new words used. The word "Kundabuffer" is invented and so is the word "Sinkrpoosaram," but that is about all. There are other chapters where literally hundred of strange words are used, so that at first glance a whole page may seem unreadable. But this difficulty quickly disappears, and the relatively few important and necessary new words become familiar. In some chapters entirely new ideas are developed with regard to "work on oneself." This applies particularly to the chapter entitled "The Holy Planet Purgatory," which Gurdjieff himself described as the heart of his writing. I must also mention the spirit of profound piety that pervades the whole book and of which you will have caught a glimpse in the extract I just quoted.

In some ways, the most significant feature of the philosophy that underlies the whole of *Beelzebub* is the notion of "universal fallibility." The Universe is presented as subject to laws—but the very nature of these laws is that an element of uncertainty enters with the act of creation itself. The history of the Earth is conceived in terms of a vast miscalculation that can only be partially remedied by intervention from "Above," that is, by messengers or prophets sent by God Himself.

I have spoken mainly about the first two books of the first series. The last part of the book consists mainly of criticism of the contemporary life of Europe and America. There are some very vivid pictures. As explained in the introduction, the intention that Gurdjieff follows in this book is to appeal not only to the mind, or even to the mind of feelings, but also to our power of visualizing and evoking concrete pictures for ourselves. Everything throughout the book is illustrated by stories and such pictures, even where very abstract principles are involved. These sometimes produce a most extraordinary effect—for example, a discussion on the nature of electricity and the nature of matter generally and of the higher energies in man is illustrated by a fantastic story of experiments carried out on the planet Saturn by beings living there who are supposed to have studied and understood the nature of this transformation of matter.

Nobody reading this book can fail to see that beneath all this strange mode of presentation, there is the very deep and serious standpoint that places in a much truer perspective than I think any other book of which I am aware the human situation and the relation of man to the universe and to God. The book is not concerned with showing the practical methods of work, but at the same time, no one can read it attentively without finding out a great deal about this. From time to time, Beelzebub gives advice to Hassein as to what he should do, which we can easily see is applicable to our own work, our own states.

When the whole narrative part of the book is finished, contained in 47 chapters, there is a postscript, called "From the Author." This now leaves on one side the story of Beelzebub and introduces and then quotes at length from a lecture presented by Gurdjieff in New York in 1924. This forms the transition to the second series in that there is introduced a great deal of material of the utmost interest and value connected with human psychology and the nature and destiny of man. Just to show you a bit about this transition, I am going to quote you what is called "The Addition." When this lecture was given in New York in 1924, Mr. Gurdjieff himself intervened at a certain point and described human nature very much on those same lines as I described in the last lecture:

At this point, I interrupted the lecturer and considered it opportune to make the following addition:

THE ADDITION

Such is the ordinary average man—an unconscious slave of the whole entire service to all-universal purposes, which are alien to his own personal individuality.

He may live through all his years as he is, and as such be destroyed forever.

But at the same time Great Nature has given him the possibility of being not merely a blind tool of the whole of the entire service to these all-universal objective purposes but, while serving Her and actualizing what is foreordained for him—which is the lot of every breathing creature—of working at the same time also for himself, for his own egoistic individuality.

The possibility was given also for service to the common purpose, owing to the fact that, for the equilibrium of these objective laws, such relatively liberated people are necessary.

Although the said liberation is possible, nevertheless whether any particular man has the chance to attain it— this is difficult to say.

There are a mass of reasons which may not permit it, and moreover which in most cases depend neither upon us personally nor upon great laws, but only upon the various accidental conditions of our arising and formation, of which the chief are heredity and the conditions under which the process of our "preparatory age" flows. It is just these uncontrollable conditions which may not permit this liberation.

The chief difficulty in the way of liberation from whole entire slavery consists in this, that it is necessary, with an intention issuing from one's own initiative and persistence, and sustained by one's own efforts, that is to say, not by another's will but by one's own, to obtain the eradication from one's presence both of the already fixed consequences of certain properties of that something in our forefathers called the organ Kundabuffer, as well as of the predisposition to those consequences which might again arise.

In order that you should have at least an approximate understanding of this strange organ with its properties, and also of the manifestations in ourselves of the consequences of these properties, we must dwell a little longer upon this question and speak about it in somewhat greater detail.

Great Nature, in Her foresight and for many important reasons (about which theoretical explanations will be given in later lectures), was constrained to place within the common presences of our remote ancestors just such an organ, thanks to the engendering properties of which they might be protected from the possibility of seeing and feeling anything as it proceeds in reality.

Although this organ was later "removed" also by Great Nature from their common presences, yet owing to a cosmic law expressed by the words "the assimilation of the results of oft-repeated acts"—according to which law, from the frequent repetition of one and the same act there arises in every "world concentration" under certain conditions a predisposition to produce similar results—this law-conformable predisposition which arose in our forefathers was transmitted by heredity from generation to generation, so that when their descendants in the process of their ordinary existence established numerous conditions which proved to be congenial for the said law-conformableness, from that time on the consequences of the various properties of this organ arose in them, and being assimilated owing to transmission, by heredity from generation to generation, they ultimately acquired almost the same manifestations as those of their ancestors.

An approximate understanding of the manifestations in ourselves of these consequences may be derived from a further fact, perfectly intelligible to our Reason and beyond any doubt whatever.

All of us, people, are mortal and every man may die at any moment.

o   o   o

If the average contemporary man were given the possibility to sense or to remember, if only in his thought, that at a definite known date, for instance, tomorrow, a week, or a month, or even a year or two hence, he would die and die for certain, what would then remain, one asks, of all that had until then filled up and constituted his life?

Everything would lose its sense and significance for him. What would be the importance then of the decoration he received yesterday for long service and which had so delighted him, or that glance he recently noticed, so full of promise, from the woman who had long been the object of his constant and unrewarded longing, or the newspaper with his morning coffee, and that deferential greeting from the neighbor on the stairs, and the theater in the evening, and rest and sleep, and all his favorite things—of what account would they all be?

They would no longer have that significance which had been given them before, even if a man knew that death would overtake him only in five or six years.

The passages I have quoted have perhaps conveyed a sense of undue emphasis in the description of the organ Kundabuffer in proportion to the whole. At the same time, it occupies a very important part in the exposition of these ideas—that is, that man is not simply an incomplete being who has something to do in order to become complete, but he is a being who has, as it were, his hands tied behind him. He begins with a handicap. He is unable to see things as they really are and therefore has not a fair start and for this reason must have help.

In the concluding pages Gurdjieff turns towards the future and sets down the task that confronts those who have realized their responsibility towards coming generations. Everyone who is prepared to make the prodigious effort required must be prepared to sacrifice all personal comfort and all personal aspirations in order to become a master to his fellows—a master who is the servant of all and whose authority rests solely on his greater capacity for effort and self-sacrifice. The last page sets down Gurdjieff's intentions with regard to the publication of his writings. It gives a hint of the most intimate and personal style of writing which he will adopt in the second series:

> It is now still midday, and as I have given my word that I would not, beginning only from tomorrow, write anything further for this first series, I still have time and shall not be breaking my word if I add with a clean conscience that a year or two ago, I had categorically decided to make only the first series of my published writings generally accessible, and as regards the second and third series, to make them not generally accessible, but to organize their distribution in order, among other things, to actualize through them one of the fundamental tasks I have set myself under essence-oath; a task which consists in this: ultimately also to prove, without fail, theoretically as well as practically, to all my contemporaries, the absurdity of all their inherent ideas concerning the suppositious existences of a certain "other world" with its famous and so beautiful "paradise" and its so repugnant "hell"; and at the same time to prove theoretically and afterwards without fail to show practically, so that even every "complete victim" of contemporary education should un-

derstand without shuddering and know, that Hell and Paradise do indeed exist, but only not there "in that world," but here beside us on Earth.

After the books of the first series have all been published, I intend, for the spreading of the contents of the second series, to organize in various large centers simultaneous public readings accessible to all.

And as regards the real, indubitably comprehensible, genuine objective truths which will be brought to light by me in the third series, I intend to make them accessible exclusively only to those from among the hearers of the second series of my writings who will be selected from specially prepared people according to my considered instructions.

Now we can turn, rather more briefly, to the books of the second series, *Meetings With Remarkable Men*. These are written in a form that is about as different as possible from *Beelzebub*. They are personal and autobiographical. They describe very simply the story of Gurdjieff's own childhood, the remarkable men whom he met and from whom he derived the point of view, the knowledge, the understanding of methods and so on, on which his own system has been based. It starts with his own father, his first tutor, and continues to describe his travels in different countries and the formation of a small group called the "Seekers of Truth," which I referred to in the second lecture. The chapter entitled "My Father" is deeply informed with filial piety that finds its counterpart in Ouspensky's description in *In Search of the Miraculous* of Gurdjieff's last visit to his father's home.

I referred in the second lecture to the influence of the dean of Kars. I may quote a short passage from the chapter entitled "My First Tutor:"

I also very well remember that on another occasion the father dean said:

'In order that at responsible age a man may be a real man and not a parasite, his education must without fail be based on the following ten principles.

'From early childhood there should be instilled in the child:

Belief in receiving punishment for disobedience.
Hope of receiving reward only for merit.
Love of God—but indifference to the saints.
Remorse of conscience for the ill-treatment of animals.
Fear of grieving parents and teachers.
Fearlessness towards devils, snakes, and mice.
Joy in being content merely with what one has.
Sorrow at the loss of the goodwill of others.
Patient endurance of pain and hunger.
The striving early to earn one's bread.'

These early chapters convey the conditions of education and early training that Gurdjieff conceives to be necessary for the men and women of the future. The real force of the second series of writings consists in this: that throughout these narratives of actual travels and meetings with "remarkable men," there emerges a realization of what was actually involved in seeking and finding the knowledge upon which Gurdjieff's teaching is based.

Before attempting to give you an explanation of the aim and significance of the second series, I propose to quote you a typical passage describing one of the meetings. It is dedicated to one of Gurdjieff's lifelong friends, Professor Skridlov, professor of archaeology at the universities of Kazan and Moscow. This is a description of a journey that he and Skridlov made together going up the old River Amu Darya, formerly called the Oxus, where they went disguised—Gurdjieff himself as a Seïd, or descendant of the Prophet Mohammed, and Skridlov as a Hadji dervish, this being a Muslim country. Their travels finally brought them into contact with a Father Giovanni, an old man living in a monastery in Kafiristan where they stayed for six months.

We lived there as we wished, and went everywhere in the monastery freely, except in one building where the chief sheik lived and to which were admitted each evening only those adepts who had attained preliminary liberation.

With Father Giovanni we went almost every day to the place where we had sat together the first time we came to the monastery, and there had long talks with him.

During these talks Father Giovanni told us a great deal about the inner life of the brethren there and about the principles of daily existence connected with this inner life; and once, speaking of the numerous brotherhoods organized many centuries ago in Asia, he explained to us a little more in detail about this World Brotherhood, which any man could enter, irrespective of the religion to which he had formerly belonged.

As we later ascertained, among the adepts of this monastery there were former Christians, Jews, Mohammedans, Buddhists, Lamaists, and even one Shamanist. All were united by God the Truth.

All the brethren of this monastery lived together in such amity that, in spite of the specific traits and properties of the representatives of the different religions, Professor Skridlov and I could never tell to which religion this or that brother had formerly belonged.

Father Giovanni said much to us also about faith and about the aim of all these various brotherhoods. He spoke so well, so clearly, and so convincingly about truth, faith and the possibility of transmuting faith in oneself, that once Professor Skridlov, deeply stirred, could not contain himself and exclaimed in astonishment:

'Father Giovanni! I cannot understand how you can calmly stay here instead of returning to Europe, at least to your own country, Italy, to give the people there if only a thousandth part of this all-penetrating faith which you are now inspiring in me.

'Eh! my dear Professor,' replied Father Giovanni,' it is evident that you do not understand man's psyche as well as you understand archaeology.

'Faith cannot be given to man. Faith arises in a man and increases in its action in him not as the result of automatic learning, that is, not from any automatic ascertainment of height, breadth, thickness, form and weight, or from the perception of anything by sight, hearing, touch, smell or taste, but from Understanding.

'Understanding is the essence obtained from information intentionally learned and from all kinds of experiences personally experienced.

'For example, if my own beloved brother were to come to me here at this moment and urgently entreat me to give him merely a tenth part of my understanding, and if I myself wished with my whole being to do so, yet I could not, in spite of my most ardent desire, give him even the thousandth part of this understanding, as he has neither the knowledge nor the experience which I have quite accidentally acquired and lived through in my life.

'No, Professor, it is a hundred times easier, as it is said in the Gospels, "for a camel to pass through the eye of a needle" than for anyone to give to another the understanding formed in him about anything whatsoever.

'I formerly also thought as you do and even chose the activity of a missionary in order to teach everyone faith in Christ. I wanted to make everyone as happy as I myself felt from faith in the teachings of Jesus Christ. But to wish to do that by, so to say, grafting faith on by words is just like wishing to fill someone with bread merely by looking at him.

'Understanding is acquired, as I have already said, from the totality of information intentionally learned and from personal experiencings; whereas knowledge is only the automatic remembrance of words in a certain sequence.

'Not only is it impossible, even with all one's desire, to give to another one's own inner understanding, formed in the course of life from the said factors, but also, as I recently established with certain other brothers of our monastery, there exists a law that the quality of what is perceived by anyone when another person tells him something, either for his knowledge or his understanding, depends on the quality of the data formed in the person speaking.'

The second series of Gurdjieff's writings contains many such accounts of meetings and conversations with "remarkable men." Each chapter is generally devoted to one of the members of the group, "Seekers of Truth," whose attitude and manifestations typify a characteristic mode of approach to this work. The stories of the journeys are themselves full of subtle teaching upon human relationship, upon the study of human nature, and upon "work on oneself."

On the title page of *Beelzebub*, the aim of the second series is stated: "To acquaint the reader with the material required for a new creation and to prove the soundness and good quality of it." In order to grasp how this aim is achieved, it is necessary to distinguish between the outer and the inner life of man. The material required for a new creation enters through our outer world and is made one's own, "transubstantiated"—to use a term often employed by Beelzebub—by work and struggle in our inner world. The second series is concerned with demonstrating that the necessary material can in fact be found in the outer world by those who are prepared to seek with sufficient persistence and determination.

By describing the "remarkable men" who participated in the search and the even more remarkable men whom they found and from whom they acquired the "material for a new creation," Gurdjieff enables the reader to form his own judgment as to the significance and value of what was done. But this judgment must be based on *external* evidence, for *internal* evidence is only established by the work itself. For this reason, the conversations and practical demonstrations in the course of which real knowledge was conveyed to the "Seekers of Truth" are usually described in terms of the external incidents only. There are one or two exceptions, notably in the chapter devoted to Ekim Bey, a

Turkish doctor and hypnotist who was from boyhood a friend of Gurdjieff and for many years a member of the "Seekers of Truth." In this chapter, a description is given of the meeting with a Persian dervish with whom they had many conversations. Gurdjieff recounts in some detail their first talk, in which the dervish gives practical advice of the greatest interest and value in connection with right and wrong work with the physical body.

In most cases, notably in the accounts of his periods of study in various monasteries and brotherhoods such as that of Father Giovanni, Gurdjieff is silent both as to the contents and the methods of the teaching that they received. In several passages he suggests that this inner aspect of their search will be made known in the third series. Altogether, in the second series there is very little reference to Gurdjieff's own inner world, that is, to his own personal reactions to the experiences and adventures of the "Seekers of Truth." These chapters give a vivid picture of his companions and their journeys—but the reader looks at the scene through Gurdjieff's eyes and does not see Gurdjieff himself.

The third series* follows just the opposite course. It is through and through *a personal record of inner experience*. It describes the events of Gurdjieff's life over a period of 40 years. Some of these events are already known to the reader from the second series—or even may have occurred during the period of his own contact with Gurdjieff and his work. A new light is thrown on all that occurred, by the revelation of his own inner experiences. We see from these writings how there was, over 40 years of struggling, a gradual emergence and clarification of the aim and significance of Gurdjieff's own life. This is not stated explicitly, but the attentive reader can see how the conception of his own task passed through the stages of the necessity to *know*, the necessity to *be*, and the necessity to *do*.

The third series cannot be understood by someone who has not immersed himself in *Beelzebub* and *Remarkable Men*. But if this preparation has been rightly conducted, the study of the third series produces on the reader an extraordinary direct effect

---

* [*Life is real only then, when "I am."*]

on the decision and power to make these efforts to *work on one-self*. Certainly, to my mind, no one has ever before succeeded in transmitting in written form the nature of this inner effort that is required to such a degree as is done in this third series of writings. Of course, it is not concerned only with our own personal inner world, but very much also with our relationships with other people, with the conditions that govern the right and wrong works of groups of people seeking the same aim, and, in a larger sense, with what is involved in bringing into the world a positive force that will create a new world.

You will understand that I cannot quote for you anything illustrative of the third series of writings, nor would it be right for me to go into them in any detail. Indeed, it would not be profitable if I did, because people who approach the third series externally do not see what it is they draw from it. They may be very much impressed or they may fail to see any significance at all, because it is not easy to convey what work on oneself really means. Most people have no inner life in the true sense of the term. Their activity is outwards, and inwardly they are passive. The great task before us all is to rediscover the true significance of the inner life of man—not for its own sake or to take refuge there from the tribulations of the outer life—but because it is only the man who is inwardly alive who can play his part in the great work that lies before us. One thing and one thing only can save mankind from destruction, and that is to arouse people from the illusion that nothing exists and nothing matters but the outer life of man. Those who are sunk in this illusion live like animals and perish like animals. Those who begin to escape from it realize that *Life is real only then, when "I am."* This is the secret of right living on this earth, and it is the secret of immortality.

O

O

JOHN GODOLPHIN BENNETT spent all of his adult life researching the nature of man and the possibility of "transformation." In 1945 he founded the Institute for the Comparative Study of History, Philosophy and the Sciences at Coombe Springs in England, where students gathered, under his direction, to study the "System" brought from the East by G.I. Gurdjieff, together with spiritual techniques used by other contemporary Sufi, Buddhist, Christian and Hindu teachers.

In 1970, seeing that a growing number of people were searching for a genuine spiritual experience and were beginning to show concern for our increasingly endangered planet, Bennett decided to intensify the work being carried on by the Institute and inaugurated the International Academy for Continuous Education at Sherborne House in the village of Sherborne in Gloucestershire, England. The Academy was a five year experiment* in passing on techniques for spiritual transformation and in awakening real conscience.

It was during this "experiment" that J.G. Bennett gave the talk appended here. *Gurdjieff Today*** was the first of seven important monographs by Bennett published under the series title, *The Transformation of Man*. Bennett Books reprints it here as a supplement, because we believe it will further urge you, the reader, to reflect more deeply on the question: *Is There "Life" on Earth?*

Bennett Books Sherborne House Editions presents material given out by J.G. Bennett during the years of the Sherborne experiment. The first book in this series, *Sacred Influences: Spiritual Action in Human Life* [Santa Fe, New Mexico], was published in May 1989. The second, *Needs of a New Age Community: Talks on Fourth Way Schools and Spiritual Community* (revised and expanded), will be published January 1990.
** *Gurdjieff Today*. Sherborne, England: Coombe Springs Press, 1974.

Appendix

Gurdjieff Today

Introduction

OUR WORK AT SHERBORNE aims at leading us to "transformation," that is, the unification of the natural and spiritual elements of our being by breaking through the barrier of illusion that keeps them apart. We are aware that mankind is entering a most critical period of history, when all will depend upon our ability to respond to the spiritual forces that seek to help us. In this, transformed men and women will be needed as never before in history. Those who feel the truth of this wish to complete their transformation quickly in order to serve the needs of mankind. For this, all possible means must be employed.

At Sherborne, the work seeks to penetrate to all parts of our nature. By learning practical skills, by taking part in all domestic duties, by working at the Gurdjieff "movements" and exercises, we develop our functions—bodily, emotional and intellectual. By struggling with our negative features, we strengthen our will. We also seek to follow Gurdjieff's advice to "learn ever more and more about the Laws of World Maintenance and World Creation." More than ever, at the present time, it is necessary for us to seek to understand the world in which we live. It is there that we must work and fulfill the tasks for which we exist as three-brained beings.

We study the world first through experience and observation, then through books, and finally through talks and discussions. Conversation or *sohbet* is one of the five means by which a Sufi teacher works with his pupils. The true name for a pupil is *Salik* or "seeker," which means "seeker of the true." Some have active intellectual powers and a good training; others have a natural, lively curiosity. For them, it is easy to engage in the study of the Laws of World Maintenance and World Creation. Those who lack, or imagine they lack, these advantages must have confidence that they can arrive by another route. The Laws are not, in their essence, hard to grasp. They are exemplified in all that we do and in all that happens about us. They can be better grasped in practice than in theory. The scientist or philosopher does not think in terms of universal analogies or cosmic Laws; he may even be repelled by the appearance of ideas that, if only he would entertain them, could revolutionize his understanding of the world.

The present booklet is the first of a series. The text is based on a lecture given at Caxton Hall, London in December 1973. It is intended for those already acquainted with Gurdjieff's ideas or other Sufi teachings. The same will apply to later booklets. Some of these will similarly discuss a single theme, such as "Energies," the "Laws of Three and Seven," or the "Second Body of Man," and others will consist of two or three talks on themes proposed week by week for study by the Sherborne students.

If these talks reach the hands of seekers who have no previous knowledge of these ideas and they find them interesting enough to provoke further inquiry, they should write to Coombe Springs Press at Sherborne House, Sherborne, Gloucestershire, England. There are hundreds of groups in many parts of the world who are seeking to prepare themselves for the coming time of troubles. However differently these groups may view the situation and however conflicting their detailed allegiances may appear to be, they need to know one another and share as far as possible their experience and understanding. There is no exclusive way to the truth—no, not even one "best" way, though each of us may think so. The Work, like Nature, produces a vast multitude of seeds and scatters them abroad to ensure that however many may fall by the wayside, the harvest will come at the time of reaping. We must nurture our own seed but not for that neglect the others.

—J.G. Bennett
Sherborne, 1973.

* [Coombe Springs Press, the original publisher of *The Transformation of Man Series,* is no longer actively publishing; Sherborne House, which was sold several years after Bennett's death in 1974, is now an apartment building.]

Gurdjieff Today

VERY YOUNG CHILDREN, two or three years old, often begin to ask the question "Why?" Sometimes they even ask the question "Why am I here?" Or, if they get the idea of life, they say, "Why am I alive?" Because people do not know how to answer such questions they put them off with foolish answers, and soon children stop asking the question "Why?" Probably they do not grasp the depth and difficulty of the question "Why?" but that they ask is an indication that somewhere deep down in us this question "Why?" is there even before we are taught anything about ourselves and the world. No one can give a convincing answer, so the question "Why?" gets gradually covered up and very few people continue to pursue it.

The man about whom I am going to speak tonight, George Gurdjieff, never gave up seeking for the answer to the question "Why?" This gives him a peculiar significance for our present time. More than ever before we are thrown back upon this question. With Gurdjieff, it never stood still. As time went on, the simple question "Why am I alive?" took the form of "Why is there life on the earth? What is this life on earth? In particular, what is our human life? What is its significance, what is it for?" Now, this question "What is our life for?" is much more unusual than you might at first notice. Because generally we have already been put off this question either by being taught that God made us and the world and it is God's business—God alone knows the answer, so it is not our business to inquire—or else we are told that there is no meaning and purpose to life except what we people bring into it. We are expected to believe that if there are purposes, they are all man-made purposes. If this were so, the answer to the question "Why do we exist?" would be "to satisfy our own purposes as they arise in us."

The second kind of answer has come to be preferred in the recent centuries, and it is the one that is still preferred at the present time. Most learned people think that any question about the sense and aim of life must be taken as a man-made question that will have a man-made answer. If so, we can virtually make whatever answer we choose.

But if we are not satisfied with that, if we can see that there is something that cannot be right in the belief that the purpose of life on earth is something man-made, then we come up against a new way of looking at the world and life. And it is that new way of looking that makes Gurdjieff's contribution distinctive. If there is a sense and purpose in human life that can be understood, that we have a part to play in fulfilling, and if this applies also to all life, then this purpose must have something to do with this earth, perhaps with this solar system, which is the world in which we live.

101

We shall then search for this answer not by going beyond this world altogether, but by looking at the world in a different way. Instead of the action of blind causes or by a divine decree coming from outside the world altogether, we shall see it as having come into being, having been designed and organized, for purposes that correspond to the size and significance of this solar system within the whole universe. So long as people could think that this earth was the centre of the universe or that our solar system was the central and most important mode of existence in the universe, they could think that all purposes were the same as the purposes of this earth and similar to purposes of man, as though he were the highest form of existence on the earth.

One of the most important changes in our view of the world has been due to the discovery that this solar system is a very insignificant item in the great universe. We see now that it would be quite absurd to think that the purposes within the solar system can be the same as those within the universe as a whole. We can say that purposes in the universe are, and are likely to remain, inscrutable to us.

But this may not be the case if we are prepared to look at the solar system in itself. Then we have to face quite a new way of looking at the problem of life. If we contemplate a purpose that is neither infinite, transcendental and beyond the universe nor confined to man and his concerns, we are bound to conclude that the purpose is limited and its attainment is hazardous. The history of the earth teaches us that in the course of evolution there have been many promising starts that have failed and left behind them only a few fossils to tell the tale. The human race—Homo sapiens—has one striking example in Neanderthal man, who for 50,000 years tried to establish viable societies and finally failed and disappeared in the arising of a new and more gifted race of men.

The consequences of thinking in terms of a limited, fallible purpose, which is nevertheless far greater than any human purpose, are prodigious. As Gurdjieff said, we may find that we are like sheep and cattle, kept only for their meat, their wool and their hides. It may turn out that man is, to use the modern phrase, "an expendable item," whose disappearance might mean a great relief to the Earth, a disappointment to the Sun, and nothing at all to the rest of the Universe.

What matters to us, however, is to learn to live with the idea that there can be purposes that are greater than human purposes and yet are infinitesimal compared with a Universal Purpose. It was this kind of reasoning that led Gurdjieff to ask his question "What is the sense and purpose of life on the earth?" When looked at in the context of the solar system, not in terms of some Absolute Reality of the universe as a whole but within this solar system, which we are, to some extent, able to study and come to terms with, it is necessary to realize that it calls for a radical change in our way of looking at our lives. We are forced to think very differently from either of the two ways that I mentioned just now.

The first answer that Gurdjieff gives to this question "What is the sense and purpose of the life on the earth, and in particular of human life?" comes from looking around us. Whenever we see that something is being taken care of on our human level, we expect to be able to answer the questions "Why are you doing this? What is this for?" Whenever we see human beings taking great care of vast herds of cattle, flocks of sheep and other animals and we ask, "What are you doing this for? Is it that you are so fond of cows and sheep that you feel you should spend so much energy in feeding them, preventing them from being destroyed by predators?" The answer is "No, no. We are taking so much care of them because we want their meat, wool and leather from them."

If we speak in the same way about mankind and ask, "What is mankind being preserved on this earth for?," what should we say? Why was so much so carefully prepared for mankind over hundreds of millions of years? Soil that has enabled this vegetation to maintain life, these various minerals that have been concentrated under the earth's surface and have enabled man to construct all the articles that he uses . . . . Why all this care? Can we examine the question as we did for our sheep and cattle? Can we say, "It is because some Higher Power is so fond of man that over hundreds of millions of years this state of affairs has been prepared?"

Supposing that we give a different answer: "No, it is not for that reason—it is because something is required from man and this human race, analogous to the requirement that we have for meat, wool and leather." That is the answer that Gurdjieff came to. It is an answer that has not been in men's minds for a very long time. Probably the last of the great teachers who taught this view of man was Zoroaster, and that was 2,500 years ago. It is implicit in the older Jewish scriptures; if one reads them impartially, one finds that such an attitude did exist in early biblical times. But now such views have been discarded.

We have such an exalted idea of man that we are not even affronted by the thought that we may, in the eyes of the Higher Powers, be no more than cattle or grass of the field that perishes. We do not even trouble ourselves to contemplate such ridiculous notions, which seem to belong to the age of savagery when man was overawed by Nature. Today, man is overawed by nothing except the vision of his own greatness.

Are we to go back to such an ancient view that man exists here to serve a limited purpose that is not of his own making? Is he here only to be used for something? When these ideas were first introduced to us by Gurdjieff 50 years ago, they were very strange—so strange and so shocking that we regarded them as intended only to jolt us, to make us sit up and ask our own question "What is my life for? What am I doing with it?" And having received this salutary jolt, then to go on living our lives, making use of what we were being taught, but not really facing the implications of the question "Are our lives for our own benefit, or do we exist to serve some purpose greater than ourselves?"

Now, at this present time, a short 50 years since Gurdjieff introduced these notions to the West, it all looks very different. Human purposes are by no means so convincing as they were before. The assumption that man knows what he is doing with his life and that he is making sense of all life on the earth is no longer plausible. We are recklessly destroying life on the earth; we are preparing considerable destruction of human life also. In the last 60 years we have destroyed unnecessarily a great deal of human life. People are very widely beginning to question human purposes and are more ready than they have been in a very long time to look at things in some new way.

Let us now try to unravel the answer to the question that Gurdjieff himself has proposed. It is that human life is required to produce "something" that is needed for the harmony of the solar system and, particularly, for the harmony of this planet and its moon. This "something" is produced by the way we live our lives and by the way we die our deaths. There is an obligation upon us to produce this "something" whether we like it or not. This "something" is analogous to the meat, wool and leather that we get from our sheep and cows.

In the past, people have had the purpose of life presented to them in different ways. But generally speaking, the way of living that has been presented as right for man has been the same. There has been a general understanding of the way that people should live. Apart from certain artificial social customs that have differed from time to time, there has been a general understanding that man is not intended to live for his own egoistic purposes, that he has obligations to fulfill and this is still as true as it has ever been.

Man has understood that he must not live like a wild or, rather, a mad animal giving way without restraint to every animal passion and egoistic impulse. He has understood that he must respect his fellow man and accept some kind of social discipline. This pattern of behaviour has been accepted as right and necessary by every kind of society and every variety of culture. What has changed very much over the ages has been the motive that has been put forward to explain why we should live in this way.

Let us take a few examples from history. Gautama Buddha appealed to reason. He said, "You see that this life is not satisfying. As it stands, it is meaningless. There is only one way out of it, and that is to awaken to the Truth, to awaken to Dharma; this is the Noble Eightfold Path. To start on the path, you must first accept a disciplined life—or moral code." This appeal to reason was powerful and effective at first, but it changed very soon and lost its power.

Then there was an appeal to faith. This is particularly in the Judaic tradition; we see it in Abraham, Moses and the psalms of David. This is God's command, and you believe it. The Jewish scriptures are concerned with strengthening this belief.

The Christian message is that we should base our life upon confidence in the love of God for man and our love for our fellow men. We should live accordingly.

Muhammad essentially put forth the doctrine of hope. The Islamic creed is one of hope. The Qur'ân is a message of hope. God is compassionate and makes no demand upon mankind that is too hard to bear. "Fulfill those simple rules of life and salvation is assured." The simple rules correspond to the way of life that is required to fulfill the purpose of our existence.

The founders of the great religions of the world have appealed to reason, to faith, to love, to hope. All of them have failed. The appeal to reason does not work. People do not, except for a small minority, live reasonably. Faith has very largely disappeared from the world. It has been replaced by a kind of blind acceptance of what we are told by a conditioning process that is totally different from real faith.

The Christian religion has been the most tragic failure of all. In the name of love more wickedness and cruelty have been perpetrated than by the followers of any other religion. Because Islam is newer than the others, it is perhaps the last to evaporate, but this religion of hope also is being replaced by motives that are totally different from those put forward by Muhammad, the founder. In short, the ways in which men have been directed towards a way of living that corresponds to our obligations on this earth have all failed.

Modern man has invented a new reason, that is, self-interest. We shall live in a certain way because it is more satisfying. We are less likely to get into trouble, we are more likely to have a "good life," if we live more or less in the same way as people have always been taught to live. The religion of self-interest is the newest of all. It rejects any other motive for right living except self-interest. But it is also the one that has collapsed the most rapidly. We are already seeing the tragic consequences of the religion of self-interest.

All of this is a paraphrase of Gurdjieff's presentation of the situation in his own books. With what does he come forward as an alternative to these ways? He says that it is necessary now for man to begin to see things as they really are. We have in us an instrument that enables us to see the truth, not indirectly through what other people have taught us, but by a direct perception. The instrument of this direct perception he calls by the ancient name of "conscience." So far I have not spoken about the "something" that man has to provide by his way of life. Now we have come to Gurdjieff's message, which is, in effect, "It is time for man to see for himself why he should live in a certain way. We must ourselves see what our lives are for, *what is the sense and significance of our existence.*"

We have come to a moment of maturing in human life, when we have to pass out of a childish dependence upon what others tell us and be able to see for ourselves. It is a very difficult moment for us when as individuals we have to "grow up." It is very much more difficult as applied to the human race as a whole. Maybe it will take centuries before we can come to it. But we are at a moment of transition when we have to learn to look at life differently—not in terms of what has been taught and believed in the past, but in terms of what we ourselves are able to see, to experience by our own direct perceptions in the present. In order to see, one must recognize what one is looking at. Therefore, some indication has to be given.

What I am now about to say is one of the most extraordinary steps in Gurdjieff's presentation. I am not aware of it having been taught before, nor that it is being taught at the present time in any other tradition. There are indications, as I said before, that it was taught by Zoroaster, that remarkable prophet of whom we know so little, and probably by Pythagoras, who according to tradition was taught by Zoroaster himself. It is not really important that it was known to a few people in the remote past, but what does matter is that it should be known now and that we should be able to see it for ourselves. Gurdjieff call it the "Doctrine of Reciprocal Maintenance."

This doctrine of reciprocal maintenance is that everything that exists in the universe depends on other things for its maintenance and must in its turn maintain the existence of others. He adds that this applies to us men also. It is very easy to see that we depend on other forms of existence. We depend on the materials of the earth's surface, upon the heat and light that come from the sun, and upon other things that we do not know about. But most of all, we depend upon *life*. We are an integral part of the life of this earth, and we cannot isolate ourselves from it. We could not eat, and in truth, we could not breathe without life on the earth, because it is the life on the earth that supplies the oxygen that makes it possible for us to breathe. Then the question comes, "If we depend upon so much for our existence, what have we got to give in return? What is required of us?"

It is not enough to say that our bodies will return to the earth, because we are a great deal more than living organisms. We cannot say that our debt to life will be paid simply by returning our carcass to the earth from which it came. What have we more? We share with all life the property of sensitivity. This sensitivity is more highly organized in us than in any other form of life. We are capable of more varied experiences. These experiences cannot be for nothing; they are not given to us for our own pleasure and suffering. Human experience releases energies that could not be produced in any other way.

To explain this in detail would take much more time than there is available tonight. Let us assume that we do recognize that human experience is different from any other form of experience on this earth. If all experience is associated with some kind of sensitive energy, then we are all producing energy. According to the kind of experience we have—which depends upon the way in which our lives are lived—we shall produce energies of different qualities. Gurdjieff asserts that certain of these are the very "something" that is required for the orderly evolution of this solar system. A great process of sensitization or, as he calls it, of spiritualization is proceeding on this earth and throughout the solar system, and we have to make our contribution to it. And we must do so by the way in which we live our lives.

We know that we take a great deal from this earth. We are beginning to see that we are taking more than we are entitled to, that we are running heavily into debt towards the earth and towards life. This makes it even more important for us to know how to repay, how to square our account with the earth and with life. We are forced to admit that we are running into bankruptcy as a human race, with debts that we shall scarcely be able to repay. This is somehow felt by people all over the world, and it makes them very uneasy about the way things are going in human societies.

We can interpret all this in ordinary terms, of exhaustion of resources and pollution and all the other things that we know about. Deeper down there is something that we suggest by such phrases as "rape of the earth," "destruction of our environment." These make us deeply uneasy, but we do not understand the full significance of it all. We may readily imagine that there are Higher Intelligences who are surveying human life and know that it is possible for man to live otherwise. Gurdjieff assures us that the Higher Powers are deeply concerned that man should live otherwise, but that they are dependent upon human understanding for this change to come about. If it is true that we people do not exist on the earth to please ourselves, or just by accident, but because we are needed for a purpose that is greater than ourselves, it must follow that if we totally fail to fulfill this purpose, we shall be removed and replaced by some other form of life.

These things that I am saying may not be as explicit as this in your mind, but I think that most of you have some feeling that there is something wrong with our present attitude towards life on the earth and towards human life in particular. There is something seriously missing in our understanding of human destiny. Therefore we should look very seriously at the answer that Gurdjieff gives.

There is a missing link. We are not seeing that our lives are required for "something." If we provide that "something" our lives will have fulfilled their purpose, and we will be set free from our debt. Our own individual fulfillment will then be made possible. This cannot be in isolation, separately from the rest of mankind, as people have sometimes thought in the past.

In olden days, it was supposed that the quest for a higher and a more significant life was a private matter that every man could pursue for himself, in solitude if need be. They thought that we should seek the company of other people only if we need them to teach us or if we feel stronger because we are sharing with others.

Such individualistic—and, indeed, egoistic—views no longer hold water. There is something here in which the whole of the human race is involved. We not only need one another, but we have an underlying connection by this very fact that the whole of the human race is needed for a certain purpose. If it fulfills this purpose, this human race of ours has the possibility of moving to a very different level of fulfillment, where a new significance can enter human life.

It is this that represents the attraction of the New World. There is a possibility for man to come to a different, differently satisfying life, providing only that people can see that this obligation of ours to provide that certain "something" is fulfilled. Then comes the question of how this is to be done.

What has Gurdjieff to say about this? In general, there is a great difference between *knowing what* and *knowing how*. At this moment, the truth is that people neither know *what*, nor *how*, to live. They feel only that there is a way in which they should live but not why they should follow this way. They see, if they are at all sensible, impartial and honest with themselves, that they are not living as they should. There is something wrong with our own behaviour which is not something we can unload on to other people. We need to know how to live our lives differently, but the first thing is to know what is this "differently." Just to live a moral, well-ordered life is not enough. We need consciously to fulfill the obligation to produce the special energies that are required from us.

The *how* Gurdjieff calls "conscious labour and intentional suffering." This phrase appears again and again in all his writings. It is necessary to understand just what he means by it. Conscious labour is nearly the same as what we should call "service." It is to serve the purpose of our existence, and this is very much concerned with the future of mankind. Throughout his own life and in every picture that he drew in his own books of the way in which life should be lived, he always emphasized the obligation we have to serve the future: to "prepare a better future for mankind." We must learn to make present sacrifices for the sake of the future.

As parents, we all see and recognize the necessity to make present sacrifices for our own children's futures. This is true, but too limited. Apart from recognition of our obligations as parents, how little remains that we are prepared to do and to sacrifice for the future. How little we are ready to do without things now, to place restraints upon our desires and impulses of the present, in order that a better future should be possible. How little do we recognize that power is not to be exercised in order to get what we want now, but in order to serve the future.

It is around such things as these that the meaning of "conscious labour" is to be understood. Why is it "conscious" labour? Because it is necessary to know what has to be done. It is an exceedingly difficult thing to serve the future rightly. Many people want to do good for the future, but they do not know what is needed. They do not know how to sow the seeds that will make a better future.

We need a change of our perceptions. Something needs to be understood that is not now understood. One of the things that has to be understood is that right living will always involve payment and sacrifice. It is not fashionable nowadays to accept the necessity for suffering, because we do not wish to admit the necessity to suffer if we are to serve. We are reluctant to give, even from our abundance—how much less when it actually hurts us. There are people I know—some of whom are in this room—who live their lives prepared to put themselves in situations where they will have to suffer in order to be of service to other people. They know that this suffering will be inevitable.

It is not enough to have the good will to serve and suffer. It is also necessary to have new kinds of perceptions, a new understanding of other people; otherwise, we are liable to blunder. With the best of intentions we can do harm and not good to other people, sow evil and not good seeds for the future. Therefore, we have also the obligation to understand human life better.

This understanding starts with the understanding of what human life is for. A great part of Gurdjieff's teaching was concerned with the study and understanding of man— not just as a being to live successfully on this earth, but essentially as a being who has obligations to fulfill and who, through fulfilling these obligations, can fulfill himself.

This is the notion of the "transformation of man." Through this, people come together. In the absence of this, people are separated. Our present life suffers terribly from isolation and loneliness. The disintegration of family life is one of the symptoms. But. in general, it is one of the sad features of our great cities that there is so much less understanding and connection between people than in the past. Our great organizations have become so impersonal that the very core of human existence is dropping away. That core is the sense of the *unity of mankind.*

We have to move towards this unity not as it was understood in the past, but in new ways. There will be changes. Something will emerge and is beginning to emerge now, in the form of new perceptions, the ability of people to communicate without words and without outward signs, through a deeper understanding and perception of one another.

There is a term that is commonly used, but it is very important to use it rightly: That is the term "group consciousness." It is used now because people are aware that in some way or other we have to get beyond our isolated and separated individualities, to the awareness of the connection between us.

I said that life by reason, life by faith, life by love and life by hope have all failed; so something else, a new kind of perception, must come that will restore these sacred qualities to their real significance in human life. We must be very careful that we do not in the same way spoil and lose the real significance of the emerging group consciousness. There is a very great risk that as the ideas that belong to the New World begin to emerge, people will take them in old ways and not see that we have to move to something quite new and different.

There is, indeed, such a thing as group consciousness. I have experienced it with many people, and we have begun to know what this really can be. We know that this is one of the new modes that will enter the New World. Group consciousness comes through the transformation of energies that are required from man, and it will make us very much more effective in the fulfillment of our obligations. I have spoken of the need to take a conscious part in the reciprocal maintenance of everything in this solar system. All this will be made more effective through group consciousness.

The most important of all is that we should be able to perceive directly, not by what other people have told us, but through the development of a new consciousness within ourselves. We should be able to see directly what the purpose of our life is, how everything is connected, how life is not separated from life, how it must be served, and how the fulfillment of our own destiny comes in doing that.

These things have been taught to us before in the form of moral rules—this is the way children are taught. "This is what you ought to do." "This is what your father tells you to do." We have to go past that and see for ourselves. Here again Gurdjieff made an enormous contribution by his long years of search through different countries of the world where he was able to come into contact with ancient groups that had at some time found and preserved the secret of this transformation of consciousness. He even saw how to develop a different kind of group awareness and to overcome the defects of our human nature. He left these techniques behind him when he died. His contribution was not only to tell what the New World will be like, but also not a little about how it can be brought about.

I have spoken up till now in terms of what Gurdjieff taught because this lecture is about him. You may feel that I have exaggerated his importance. It is not in terms of importance that I speak, but in terms of the uniqueness and the unexpectedness of his message. If you set yourself to understand this message more closely, you will see that there is something really strange that this should be so different from so much that is being said at the present time. There are so many people proclaiming the advent of the New World and telling us what man should do about it. They speak justly and rightly about new forms of consciousness and new perceptions, but they overlook the particular fact that our life must be governed by the obligation to produce something needed for the world.

Since this is connected with the way we experience, it follows that we must transform our own way of life. This is something I do not see elsewhere. Many other valuable things are being said and done that are all necessary and contribute to making the New World, but this particular teaching is the most important of all. Why is this? Because we are now coming to the point where we people have to understand what our lives are for. It is no longer enough to do what we are told nor live by the promise of something wonderful for ourselves if we do what we are told. We have to be more mature than that.

I will finish my lecture at this point and ask you if there are any things about which you would like me to speak more fully.

Questions and Answers

QUESTION. What does Gurdjieff mean by "conscious labour and intentional suffering?" How do they apply to what you have been saying?

J.G. Bennett. It is a good question, which goes to the root of the matter. I said that we have to serve the future. The simplest possible example is the relation of parent and child. When parents truly fulfill their obligations towards their children, they take on conscious labour and intentional suffering. Unless they are complete fools, they know that they will have to work and suffer. No parent who loves his children has ever not suffered. We must accept this suffering and know that our relation with our children must be one of giving and not of demanding. We must know we have to sacrifice our own self-love. We must not expect something in return from our children, and at the same time we must not avoid the suffering that will come to us through being firm with our children.

It is a very hard discipline to be a good parent. That is a characteristic example of conscious labour and intentional suffering. It requires a great deal of understanding. One cannot be a good parent merely by wanting to. However much one may love one's children, one will make mistakes unless one has set oneself to understand, to be able to enter into their experience. This is why conscious labour and intentional suffering require a change of perception.

Question. What do you think about Gurdjieff as a man? Was he as white or as black as he is painted? What was he trying to do with all his strange behaviour? You had personal contact with him—what did you make of him?

JGB. I have just written a book about Gurdjieff; as I decided to write this about him, I set myself to answer that question in 364 pages. But let me try to give a short answer to it. Gurdjieff had an exceptionally hard life, and this was largely due to his own exceptionally difficult nature. He had a great deal to overcome in himself. He had extraordinary powers that he very seldom exercised because for certain reasons he knew that he had to refrain from exercising them.

It is quite true I have had personal contact with him. I have seen that he had powers that were not ordinary, not like anyone else I have personally met. He could have lived a very comfortable life if he had chosen to make use of his powers. But on the contrary, he led throughout an extremely difficult life. He was concerned from quite an early age, from the age of 32 onwards, in seeing how he could transmit to people what he himself had been fortunate enough to learn. From 1909 to 1949, that is 40 years, he laboured to find ways of transmitting, constantly experimenting, sometimes making quite serious mistakes, but never ceasing to search right to the end of his life for ways in which he could transmit to people the things that he had been able to learn through exceptionally favourable circumstances.

You must understand that he made a distinction between "intentional suffering" and "voluntary suffering." Sometimes one can voluntarily inflict suffering on oneself in order to gain a particular result for one's benefit. An athlete will inflict suffering upon himself, undergoing severe training and exerting a great deal of self-control in order to develop his powers as an athlete. Such voluntary suffering is quite different from intentional suffering.

Intentional suffering is accepting the consequences of actions one undertakes for the benefit of others. Anyone who sincerely wishes to do something for the benefit of others must understand that this will always bring trouble on himself. It is a law that Gurdjieff understood very well. He brought a great deal of trouble on himself. Intentional suffering simply means that one accepts the consequences of one's actions, knowing that this will include painful experiences. Voluntary suffering is different. Here one is doing something for a definite purpose, in general for one's own benefit, as a miser will starve to fill his coffer.

Question. Gurdjieff's ideas have so far received little public support. Do you think that this will change? Do you see him as a prophet of the New Age?

JGB. He was certainly a precursor who saw far more clearly than most people of his time that there was something terribly wrong with the way people were living and behaving all over the world. As I read the present situation 25 years after Gurdjieff died, the time has come when it is possible to put much more effectually into practice what he taught than has been the case hitherto. That is one reason why I am speaking as I am now.

In the last two or three years, I have been making an experiment on these lines myself with a number of people at Sherborne House. I want to talk to you about that, because it is an experiment following a plan Gurdjieff himself indicated in the organization of his own institute some 50 years ago. It is for training people on the lines I have been speaking of: that is, in the development of their powers of perception, both external and internal, and in showing them how it is possible to come to group consciousness.

That is a big undertaking, and I can only attempt it with people who are able and prepared to devote themselves entirely to it for a fairly long period of time. For various reasons I decided that it needs 10 months time. I am looking for people who have the potential for developing these powers—because it is very important that those who have this potential should be prepared as soon as possible. There is a growing need for people with this capacity.

That is the task that I have set myself at Sherborne. I have been working also with a number of people in the London area, as far as possible on the same lines but without the intensive conditions. It is not possible in the short time available to tell you more than the general principles of what Gurdjieff presents to us as the way in which the New World will come about. I regard it as my duty to share with people as far as is possible for me what I myself have learned from Gurdjieff and other teachers.

Question. What is the meaning of the picture behind you with the words "Is there 'life' on the earth?"

JGB. It is the title of a book just published in America. I asked Gerald Wilde, an artist who is living with us at Sherborne—a man of extraordinary genius—to draw me something for tonight that would ask the question "Is there 'life' on the earth?" This is what he drew. It must speak for itself.

Question. What happens to people who begin to work on themselves and then give up the struggle? Isn't it worse for them than if they had never started?

JGB. I have long experience. It is more than 50 years since I first met Gurdjieff and Ouspensky. I have seen people over the greater part of their lives. I have seen people who started and appeared to have given up. Very often I later have seen that it was not true that it was worse for them. I am talking now from actual experience and observation. If something has really started in people they may give up outwardly, but something continues beneath the surface. Maybe many years later one sees that the process has not stopped in them.

In the last year of Gurdjieff's life, I remember very well a man I had known who was the first Englishman who ever met Gurdjieff in the Caucasus [Mountains] just before he came to Constantinople, where I first met him in 1920. He was a very good Russian scholar and very valuable to Gurdjieff as a translator. He was very close to Gurdjieff in the early years, but after a certain time he appeared to drop out. Things went very badly with him. But he came over to Paris in 1949 to see Mr. Gurdjieff. I was sitting on one side of Mr. Gurdjieff and he was sitting on the other, and he asked him, "I have given up—is it too late for me to start again?"

Gurdjieff said, "It is never too late. This work does not stop. If you will follow my indications now, you will find what you are looking for before you die." It was an unforgettable moment because this spanned a whole lifetime. He did indeed die well.

I have seen this more than once in my long experience. People who have apparently given up have not lost the inner working. If there is in people a genuine longing to discover the true significance of life, they may give up for external or for personality reasons; but once the seed is sown, it must continue to mature. Of course, if the contact with it was fictitious or mental only, it is another matter. If they never did anything but pretend, then no seed has been sown. Those who really give up are the ones who never started. In telling you this, I am not quoting from anyone else's books or teachings. I am talking of my own personal experience.

Question. Can you tell us if Gurdjieff expected a world catastrophe? Did he prepare for what was going to happen? Did he foresee a great fight between the powers of good and evil?

JGB. I do not think he expected the wholesale destruction of a great part of the human race. The end of the old world and the start of the new was the subject of the very last talk I had with him just a week, almost to the hour, before he died. I was with him for two hours that Saturday morning, October 22, 1949, and he was speaking about the conflict between the old world and the new. He referred to this very confrontation you have in mind, of open conflict between the East and the West, as he put it, which at that time was apparently imminent between the U.S.A. and the U.S.S.R.

He said, "This looks unavoidable, but it will not happen. This is not the real conflict, which is between the old world and the new. It is not between one form of materialism and another form of materialism. This real conflict between the old and new," he said, "is a serious one. The outcome is not guaranteed. It is now possible for the world to be 'made tchic.'" He clearly identified himself with the New World when he said, "Either I will make the old world 'tchic' or it will make me 'tchic.' Now another great war will not happen. When Beelzebub is published, a new force will come into the world."

I think we have to take into account that there is an enormous inertia in the old world, whose death we are witnessing today. In another talk I gave on this subject I spoke about dinosaurs. A hundred million years ago, life on earth was dominated by the reptiles, which reached enormous sizes. The dinosaurs were huge, small-brained, slow-moving creatures that were well adapted to the mild and stable climates of the Cretaceous Period. When the world climate changed, that dominant form of life gave up and was replaced by much more active and positive forms of life.

We are at the present moment in a *dinosaur civilization.* Enormous, slow-moving, small-brained organizations are now dominating the world. The dinosaurs gradually lost as the climate became too inhospitable for them. They became more and more helpless, and a new form of life emerged, that is, the warm-blooded mammals.

This is extraordinarily like the present situation in the world. We are dominated by large organizations, governments, churches, industrial giants, financial groups, international organizations. All these are large and they grow larger, as the dinosaurs did. It is visible to everyone that their level of intelligence and their ability to look into the future are exceedingly small. They are quite unable to adapt to the New World, but they will not give up easily. They are unable to adapt to the new climate; the climate for these big organizations was that of expansion. As long as there was room and the means to expand, they could thrive. This climate is changing, and we are entering a period when it no longer will be possible to expand. Growth will be impossible. Then it will be not merely a duty but a necessity to control, to restrain and concentrate. Under such circumstances, big organizations collapse. They can exist only in a state of expansion. This we can see. It is possible to explain just why it must be so. But this is not necessary, because we can see it for ourselves.

The New World will be dominated by active, mobile and much more intelligent forms of social life. This is why we have to look to small groups and communities; and above all to the emergence of group consciousness, which corresponds to the state of the warm-blooded animals. We need a warm-blooded society, not the present cold-blooded society.

Because of the great advantage warm blood has over cold in times of stress, I believe that the New World will survive. There will be a time of great difficulties, and it is not desirable that the collapse of the old world should come suddenly. It would probably not be possible to survive a sudden collapse of order throughout the world. Little by little the old world will die out. New social forms, new modes of existence, will take its place. For this, we must prepare ourselves today. If we have a feeling towards that, if something in us responds to that, then our first duty is to prepare.

Question.   Do you see a connection between what you have been saying and the work you are doing at Sherborne House?

JGB.   Indeed I do—a very close relationship.

Question.   How is true group consciousness achieved?

JGB.   It is necessary to pass through certain experiences together. But as I have said before, there is fictitious group consciousness and there is *real* group consciousness. To understand the difference is very important for anyone who is concerned about the society of the future. It is possible to produce an emotional excitement shared by a large number of people. This is not group consciousness but "crowd consciousness." It is quite different and really the opposite. Crowd consciousness is always wasteful, even if it is not destructive. Group consciousness is always creative. Crowd consciousness can be produced by external stimulus whereas group consciousness can be achieved only by internal change.

What we have at Sherborne House is a school modelled as far as possible on what Gurdjieff prescribed when he was laying down the organization of his own Institute for the Harmonious Development of Man. The aim is precisely that: the harmonious development of all sides of our nature. This means not only our intellectual, bodily and emotional powers but also to develop the will, which is "I," the spiritual nature of man.

For this, we have very varied activities. All kinds of skills are learned; everything is done in common. All the people living at Sherborne—there are about 120 all together—work together and go through this training. The practical skills include the work of the house, care of animals, food production, carpentry, stone masonry, and many other arts and crafts. The rapid learning of new skills, especially when they are learned by people working together in groups, develops perceptions and common understanding, thus preparing the ground for group consciousness.

We make a great deal of use of the extraordinary discoveries of Gurdjieff in the field of bodily exercises, including sacred dances and rituals. We also work on various psychological, historical and philosophical questions. We study language, art and music, so that as far as possible all sides of our nature are developed together. Ages range from 18 to 70, and the students come from 10 to 15 countries, although the majority are Americans. You can read about it in the prospectus of the Academy.

It is called the International Academy for Continuous Education to emphasize that it has an international character, and that it is for the all-round development of man. This is the idea of the Academy, and it is something for our entire lives. We do not look upon education as something one does once and for all in one's youth, but rather that the process of our harmonious development must continue, as Gurdjieff put it, until our "last breath."

Sherborne is for me the fulfillment of something that Gurdjieff spoke to me about in August 1923. He told me many things about his plans and how he hoped his institute would develop. I was particularly fortunate because I could speak Turkish nearly as well as English. Gurdjieff could speak Turkish perfectly because it was the lingua franca of the part of the world where he grew up. I was able to talk more with him than most visitors, so I was able to learn from him all that he chose to tell me about his ideas for the future. These have remained with me, and it was an extraordinary opportunity that came only about three years ago to be able to put a great deal of that into practice and see how it worked. It is remarkable to see how well he foresaw so long ago what would be needed. He did say that this would come in the future.

Question.   Can you tell me more about Gurdjieff and his life? I have read many of the books but have the impression that we have not heard the whole story. Why did his institute not continue and develop at that time?

JGB.   Ostensibly, Gurdjieff's Institute for the Harmonious Development of Man folded up owing to an almost fatal motor accident in July 1924. You must realize that he was at an enormous disadvantage, because, although he spoke many Eastern languages, at that time he could hardly speak any European language. He depended upon interpreters. When, in addition, he was nearly killed by this frightful accident, he just could not continue. He was forced to abandon all his plans for the Institute, and instead put his ideas in writing. That is how his books came to be written. There were also deeper reasons that Gurdjieff discloses in the third series of his writings.

Question.   Can you tell us how your work and that of Idries Shah are connected? Is he interested in Sherborne House?

JGB.   Shah has his work to do, and I have mine. They are different and scarcely overlap at all. Shah is stirring people up very effectively all over the world. He is making them think, showing them that modes of thought that appear to be free are really psychologically conditioned. He has the cooperation and support of scholars, scientists and men of action all over the world. He is doing a very important work on a much larger scale than anything that I am attempting. It aims at awakening people to the absurdity and also the gravity of the present situation and of giving people hope of a way out. It is a direct action that concerns the immediate future of mankind. I said to somebody today that I regard Shah as the Krishnamurti of Sufism. As Krishnamurti goes about breaking down people's fixed ideas, so is Shah doing a good deal to break down people's illusions. This is a very necessary preparation for the New World.

What I am trying to do is to take people who have enough determination and aptitude to go through a fairly rigorous training and prepare themselves to serve the world in its process of transformation. So that my task is a quite different one, it is directed to a more distant future of 10, 20 or even 50 years hence.

Question.   It seems to me that what you are saying is very close to what Idries Shah and the Sufis are saying.

JGB.   It is very close. A great part of Gurdjieff's ideas came from Sufi sources. But I think you will see that this particular thing that I have been talking about today is not to be found in any Sufi literature you know about. There is another, probably more ancient, tradition along side the Sufi tradition in which this knowledge was transmitted. It is known as the Sarman Brotherhood. It was not until Gurdjieff found this Sarman tradition that he really saw the answer to his question "What is the sense and significance of human life?"

You must understand that "Sufi tradition" is a broad term. If we speak of the "Christian tradition," we know that we have to make an important distinction between Eastern and Western Christianity. It is not only a matter of doctrine, but of the way in which the spiritual life is understood in the East and the West. There are also great differences within Islam and particularly in Sufism. Whereas Islamic doctrine tells the believer *what* he must do, Sufism tells him *how* to do it.

In my personal opinion, after long years of study and having met many Sufis in many parts of the world, the core of Sufi tradition comes from Central Asia. There is a very ancient source from which many traditions have originated: Vedic, Avestan or Zoroastrian, Buddhist, Mithraic, and much of Judaism and Christianity. Before Sufism entered Islam, Buddhism was the dominant tradition in Central Asia. That is why the true Central Asian Sufism is as much Buddhist as it is Islamic.

Question.   You speak about the possibility of acquiring new perceptions.

Where does this power come from? How could I know whether I have it or not?

JGB.   All people have it. That is how man is made. We are endowed with this possibility just as much as we are with the possibility of touching and smelling and seeing; indeed, more so, because one can be born blind, but one is not born without this possibility. It is inherent in the very essence of human nature, but that does not mean that everyone has an equal chance of achieving it. Not at all. That may vary greatly between one person and another. How far people can go also varies enormously. Those who are able to go all the way are the rarest of the rare. That is how it is arranged. But everyone has the potential to realize or neglect—it is a matter of our own choice. That is said in the new law of Moses: "Behold, I set before you this day life and death, blessing and cursing. Choose therefore life that thou and thy seed may live."

I am personally concerned—my task is to find people who have a high potential and help them to realize it. That does not mean that there is not much to be done for everyone but if people who have a high potential will be prepared to accept "conscious labour and intentional suffering," they can then become the means of help to many others beside themselves. This is really the principle: If you are able to receive much, you are also able to give much.

Question.   Do people who go to Sherborne all get this?

JGB.   This is now beginning to emerge. The people who came in the first year in 1971 have now been able to see what they are able to do. I myself am very satisfied. By no means all of them could continue independently, but a certain number are able to and are at this present time able to share with others something of what they received during their Basic Course.

This is happening in different parts of the world. In all of this you must understand that I have been guided by the pattern that Gurdjieff laid down. He intended that people who went through a training at his central institute should afterwards be able to go to different places and pass on what they had received.

Question.   Is there a chance of saving the world from disaster?

JGB.   The old world is past saving. During this present century the first great disaster has already occurred. This was due to the failure of mankind to recognize the enormous responsibility we incurred through our great technical discoveries, especially the release of energy through steam, internal combustion engines and electrical generators. This release of energy threw the world out of balance. Only conscious people could have rectified it.

According to Gurdjieff, there was a group in Tibet who could have saved the world, but their leader was killed by a stray bullet when the British invaded Tibet in 1902, and the rest of the group died soon after. This group knew the secret of generating spiritual energies needed to neutralize the destructive forces released by our technical discoveries. Gurdjieff had learned a part of this secret and passed it on to us. It is the answer to his question "What is the sense and significance of human life on this earth?"

Because of the disaster in 1902, the world collapsed. Two world wars and the loss of 40 million lives were the visible consequences. The breakdown of human societies and the threat of a third world war were before us in 1950, but strange things happened that averted the final tragedy.

Now we must think of saving the New World. We continue to make technical discoveries and release more and more energy. If we succeed in harnessing the energy of atomic fusion, a really frightful situation will arise. The work started in Tibet 100 years ago will have to be resumed on a far greater scale.

To save the world, three different kinds of action are required: One is visible and two are invisible. The visible work is to prepare the new social order. We shall need "work communities" or, as Gurdjieff called them, "fourth way schools." These will be devoted to training people to survive and perfect themselves under the severe conditions of the next 100 years. These schools will have the practical task of creating self-supporting communities able to work together and share resources and also to help their environment. This is much harder than it looks.

Modern man is a taker and not a giver. Whoever has power uses it to take and hold, whereas the only right use of power is to give and share with others. It is possible to go far enough in the elimination of egoistic grasping after one's own benefit to be able to live and work in a community. But this requires teaching and training. That is what fourth way schools are for, but only on the exoteric or outer plane.

The deeper mesoteric work is concerned with energies. Psychic and spiritual energies must be released, concentrated, stored up and put to work in the right way. This requires very special knowledge and readiness to work and sacrifice. There are schools in the world that are doing this today, but they are not in the West. We need to take up this work ourselves.

If people are willing to undertake such work, they must first be tested to see if they have the required qualities. They must be able to put aside personal ambition and set themselves to serve the future without expectation of reward. Gurdjieff once said that 200 conscious people could stop war. If this number will be available by 1990, the disaster that threatens mankind will be averted.

At Sherborne we have made a start, and already a few people are on the way. In 1977, I hope to have a special course for those who have prepared themselves. If all goes well, we shall contribute our quota to the group of energy transformers. There are other centres where similar preparations are going on.

Finally, there is the true esoteric work, which is supernatural. There is at this present time a great spiritualizing action that is preparing the New Epoch. This action comes, as Gurdjieff puts it, "from Above." All we can do is to cooperate with it and be its instruments. The spirit cannot work without the flesh. The New World communities are the flesh of the new humanity. Spiritual energies are its blood, but its life is entering from Above.

I have confidence that this action will succeed and that many of you here today will see the birth of the New World.

O